HEART CRIES OF EVERY TEEN

Eight Core Desires That Demand Attention

Jackie E. Perry, MS, LPCS

Kate,

May God richly bless you as you care for your heart while pursuing the hearts of others!

Jackie Perry

 Straight Street Books
Lighthouse Publishing of the Carolinas

HEART CRIES OF EVERY TEEN: EIGHT CORE DESIRES
THAT DEMAND ATTENTION BY JACKIE E. PERRY
Published by Straight Street Books
An imprint of Lighthouse Publishing of the Carolinas
2333 Barton Oaks Dr., Raleigh, NC 27614

ISBN: 978-1-64526-248-0
Brought to you by the creative team at Lighthouse Publishing of the Carolinas (lpcbooks.com): Eddie Jones, Cindy Sproles, Betty Hassler, Brian Cross, and Judah Raine

Any Web addresses or links in this book may have changed since publication and may no longer be valid. Stories with names and identifying details have been changed to protect the privacy of individuals.

Library of Congress Cataloging-in-Publication Data
Perry, Jackie E.
Heart Cries of Every Teen: Eight core desires that demand attention /
Jackie E. Perry, MS, LPCS/ 1st ed.

Printed in the United States of America

PRAISES FOR *HEART CRIES OF EVERY TEEN*

For decades, Jackie E. Perry has come alongside adolescents and parents in her counseling practices. In *Heart Cries of Every Teen,* she shares eye-opening insights and practical applications through an easy to understand framework. This book is a treasure chest of wisdom. It belongs on the shelf of every youth worker, counselor, and parent of teenagers. If you want to better understand the teenagers in your life, here's your "go-to" resource!

~Drew Hill
Pastor and award-winning author of
Alongside: Loving Teenagers with the Gospel

Heart Cries of Every Teen should be on the nightstand of every parent and a go-to present for every mom and dad. This is the *What to Expect When You're Expecting* equivalent for rearing teens! If you want to figure out what your teenager's heart is longing to hear, then wrap your arms around this book!

~Angela Pisel
Author of *With Love From The Inside* and *The Patient*

Thank you, Jackie Perry, for writing *Heart Cries of Every Teen*—a "must-read" for parents, pastors, educators, youth leaders, therapists—anyone wanting to understand and impact adolescents. This brilliant integration of transparency, wisdom, and encouragement honors the complex physical, spiritual, emotional, psychological and neurobiological world of adolescence.

~**Judith Stewart**
LPCS and Co-Founder
Cornerstone Counseling Center, Hickory, NC

Through real-life accounts, psychological facts, biblical wisdom, and practical recommendations, this exceptional resource equips parents to look beyond the surface of their teen's behavior and into his/her heart. Jackie's knowledge coupled with her insights provides hope and help, removing some of the mystery that parenting teenagers involves. This book will impact lives—for now and eternity.

~**Emily Wickham**
Mom of four and founder
Proclaiming Him to Women Ministries

Jackie Perry has brought what can seem like complicated adolescent issues into a whole new light in very relatable ways. At the same time, she highlights the spiritual component that is so often lacking in books addressing these issues. Her very smooth, engaging writing will help so many parents!

~**Karen Dagher**
editor and ghost writer

The author's meshing of her professional experience, vital clinical information, and biblical truth is seamless and engaging. From the mind and the heart, she provides a comprehensive framework of the challenges of adolescence. The book gives solid biblical counsel—without ever being preachy or churchy—and without simplistic bromides that frankly are in lots of Christian books. Maybe it's the YL leader in me, but I fell in love with the kids whose stories she tells.

~**Tom Hammon**
Vice President of Young Life,
UK/Ireland/Scandinavia

This resource is SO timely, helpful, biblical, and balanced. The quest to look deeper than a teen's words and behaviors to the heart cries below is critical for every parent and mentor—and also transferable to other relationships. This is no academic work of armchair theology or psychology. This book is wisdom from the trenches.

~**Bob Thompson**
Pastor, Corinth Reformed Church, Hickory, NC
President, Faithful and Welcoming Churches (UCC)

As a parent of two teen boys I found *The Heart Cries of Every Teen* to be exactly the roadmap I have been craving. The emphasis on the value of positive relationships with parents, peers and our Father—and how they can be used to satiate the desires of our hearts—

provides me a framework to have meaningful, deep and life-altering conversations with my boys. This work will prove to be a blessing to all who chose to take the journey.

~**Norm Lizarralde**
Parent of two teen boys

Dedication

To John W. Perry,
my best friend, my partner in parenting,
my greatest encourager, and
my faithful balloon man.
Thank you for believing in me.

Contents

Acknowledgments

At the Blue Ridge Christian Writer's Conference in North Carolina, I met agents David and Sarah Van Diest. With a few ideas and a strong desire to communicate what I'd learned as an adolescent counselor, I nervously yet passionately shared why parents and caring adults need to understand how core desires drive so much of the best and the worst in our kids. This early discussion fueled and formed the basis of this book. I am deeply indebted to them for their encouragement. David, thank you for being my agent, a brother in Christ, and friend.

After entering a portion of the manuscript in the Christian Writer's Conference Badge of Honor contest, I was very grateful for the publishing contract I was awarded with Lighthouse Publishing of the Carolinas. Thank you, Eddie Jones, Cindy Sproles, and the readers on the panel that selected my manuscript.

God gave me my editor, Betty Hassler, at just the right time. I am deeply indebted to you for helping me transform a long-winded and wandering manuscript into a more rhythmic and reasonable read. You know, dear Betty, I couldn't have done this without your gentle, persistent prodding combined with your words of affirmation.

I must thank my dear husband John, whose love and steadfast support, encouragement, and commitment to this project blessed me more than I can express. You are my kind "balloon man," who patiently pulls the strings tethered to this hot air balloon when I am emotionally floating off into never-never land. I love you so much.

My kids, Emily, Alex, and Sam, God bless 'em. You have grown up hearing me talk about the brain and the heart so much that I am sure you could each write a book of your own. I pray that I daily reflect the Father as I strive to care for you and your hearts. I love you three so deeply and am so grateful for our sweet family.

I also want to thank my colleagues and co-workers at Cornerstone Counseling Center. Few people have the privilege to work in such a Christ-centered environment where God's glory remains our highest goal. I appreciate the support of my directors and co-workers, especially Mike and Judy Stewart and Shirley Huffman. Thank you to all of my clients who entrusted your hearts to me as you allowed me to walk beside you for a time.

Thank you to my church family, Corinth Reformed Church in Hickory, North Carolina, where I taught the core concepts in our Parents of Teens and Students Sunday School Class for an entire quarter. Thank you especially to Bob and Linda Thompson and Paul and Danielle Cummings, our incredible pastors and their wives who prayed for me and regularly inspired me.

Thank you to encouraging and supportive friends: Kelly Duncan, Abby Pulley, Kristi Stephenson, Dana Lowry, Gayle Robinson, Elizabeth Tracy, Amy Castell, Mary Felkins, Karen Dagher, Tasha Runyon, Margaret Whisler, Becky Mercendetti, Tracey Bolick, Angie Pisel, Emily Wickham, Debbie Carlton, Sarah Kincaid, Emma Danzey Burnham, Julie McGrath, and my faithful, adorable writing companion Bailey, my mini Goldendoodle.

Few people can say they have two sets of parents who unconditionally love them and wholeheartedly support them. Thank you to my parents, German and Nora Escano, and my in-laws, Ed and Ellen Perry. Pop, I feel your presence and can imagine your words of encouragement to me every single day.

Moving to a new city in the midst of writing this book brought many challenges as well as rewards. Thank you to the ladies in my Asheville Bible study: Wyndy Bonesteel, Heather Compton, Amy Flagler, Constanza Frank, Leslie Hill, Julie Lizarralde, Lori Pinkerton, Abby Reeder, and Karen Sikkink. God gifted me with an amazing group of sisters at just the right time.

Last but not least, I am grateful for a God who loves me, leads me, and refines me through every endeavor. I got to lean into You like never before in order to string words together in a meaningful way. May You be honored and glorified as You bring insight and healing into the lives of kids and families everywhere.

Introduction

You may be reading this book because you have an immediate issue you hope to address with your teenager. You'd like quick insights and even quicker solutions. I get it. I have three kids of my own—one teenager and two young adults. I also work as an adolescent therapist. Like you, I wish I could apply a guaranteed treatment approach that will help me motivate a kid or family to change. I want this great kid to just stop it and do the right thing. I think I clearly see what should happen and too often believe I can quickly move to resolution.

Our roles as parents, teachers, mentors, and friends certainly give us a measure of wisdom and insight. However, we can easily bypass the heart of a kid in our attempt to foster peace. We see him resist limits and say, "I must reinforce this boundary and increase consequences." We see her passivity and ponder, "What can I do so she will be motivated to do X, Y, or Z." Essentially, we develop plans and programs based on very good principles. We're ready to nip things in the bud and respond to whatever comes our way.

While these strategies certainly have their place, they rarely address the depth of problems that often appear during the adolescent years. Moreover, these behavior-based methods don't typically foster connections with teens that yield more openness, honesty, and vulnerability. Even if our quick reactions may be justified and arguably are the best course of action, our sense of urgency to fix what we observe may cause us to miss out on what lies at the core of their messiest moments.

The truth remains that getting to the source of the struggle will require us to face the tension and conflict head on. I know personally and professionally that it would be much easier to win the fight or just step out of the ring altogether. Who wants to deal with the emotions that naturally arise when doors slam, kids yell, illegal activity surfaces, or any other disruption occurs? We are angry, afraid, confused, and worried—not to mention, just plain tired. These crises never seem to happen when we have the time, energy, and mental fortitude to delve deeper and devise a reasonable plan.

Out of a desperate desire for peace and restoration, we find ourselves saying something or doing something that's unhelpful, counterproductive, and even destructive. After the dust settles, the gap between our teens and us grows wider. The pathway to their hearts appears weedy and overgrown.

For many, these emotions immobilize us. Instead of reacting, we don't respond at all. We don't know what to do. So we hope and pray that they're just going through a phase. Surely, the peace and restoration we desire will come about in due time. As a result, we may cope by minimizing, dismissing, or even denying the presence of problematic patterns of behavior. Meanwhile, the disruptions continue, and perhaps even intensify, until someone visibly explodes or silently implodes.

Knowing when and how to respond can easily be the most challenging part of parenting or guiding adolescents. If we learn to consider what we see and hear as reflections of their hidden hearts, then we can begin to approach the pain, the passion, the passivity, and the pandemonium in a way that somehow ministers to this central place within them. This truth is reflected in the verse, *The good person out of the good treasure of his heart produces good, and the evil person out of his evil treasure produces evil, for out of the abundance of the heart his mouth speaks* (Luke 6:45). The heart impacts everything. An adolescent's intentions, motivations, perspectives, beliefs, feelings, attitudes, actions, and verbal and nonverbal exchanges are all influenced by the state of their hearts and the desires that form there.

Reaching and connecting with this deep place in the soul of another, especially an adolescent, can certainly feel like a climb up Mount Everest. The pursuit will take time, intention, and a great deal of trial and error. Not only that, because every kid possesses unique DNA that interacts with completely different DNA in ever-changing environments, no perfect map or tried and true method will help us navigate the landscape of the heart. But a quest to understand and connect with the heart of an adolescent is possible when it mirrors the truths of God's Word and reflects the way in which He pursues each of us.

God doesn't use a formula to reach you and me. Instead, He understands the centrality of the heart. He knows what our hearts deeply desire. He also knows how both the past and the present can taint and tame these longings. With wisdom, grace, compassion, mercy, and an immense amount of patience, God gently and persistently seeks us and satisfies our hearts in a way that far outweighs anything we could concoct on our own.

Therefore, if we can gain a basic understanding of the heart and the core desires that flow from it, we can begin to make sense of a lot of the difficulties that arise during adolescence. Combining this knowledge with grace-filled principles and practices that mirror the heart of the Father, we can actually begin to encourage, direct, and redirect them in a way that invites them to live the life God intended for them.

In the first section of this book, I paint a broad picture of the heart and soul of adolescents. For those of you who, like me, just want to get to the meat, you will find the brevity of these chapters and the metaphors they pose to be just what you need to help you recognize the importance of this central place. For the reader who wants depth on the heart of a teen, the chapters direct you to a few authors who have written extensively on this subject. Regardless, reading this first section will help you gain a sense of why the core desires of the heart matter, how developmental changes influence them, and how they in turn impact what you observe in the adolescents you know.

Section two contains a chapter on each of eight core desires of the heart. Through stories about teens and families, based on true events that I've changed to protect their identities, you will understand how each heart cry influences both positive and negative actions and attitudes. This section also offers the reader some practical ways to minister to these core desires in our kids. More importantly, it connects each desire with scriptures that help parents and kids understand how God and His community of faith can deeply satisfy each desire.

In section three I address how suffering, sin, and salvation impact these eight core desires. Since each of these desires resides within adults as well, we must assess how we are caring for our own hearts. Furthermore, if we don't have a connection with Christ and a community of others who walk beside us, we will sorely limit our ability to impact the teens in our lives.

May God guide your search for the hearts of your teens and grace you with His presence, power, and love as you journey.

Jackie Perry
Asheville, NC

Section One: Hearts Revealed

In the first section of this book, I want to broaden your understanding of the heart and soul of adolescents before I offer some practical application. The heart is central to life. I'm not referring to the physical beating organ but metaphorically to the foundational place for change within each of us. We must focus on a teen's heart and soul before we can grasp how the eight heart core desires impact his or her attitudes and actions (Section Two).

In fact, the heart is inseparable from any problem or pattern of behavior. Failure to understand this interior space may set you up to grasp for inferior or ineffective tools to deal with conflict or tension. I want you to have the proper posture and perspective. Therefore, the three chapters in this section will help you gain a sense of why the core desires of the heart matter, what influences them, and how they in turn impact the adolescents you know.

First, I will overview the heart as defined in scripture. Second, I will briefly describe the soul as it relates to the heart and adolescent development. Last, I will offer a short summary of the many changes that take place during this period in life and how these disrupt the state of the adolescent heart. In doing so, I hope you gain a better sense of why and how core desires of the heart drive so much of the good, the bad, and the ugly behaviors that typify adolescence.

Chapter 1

The Hidden Heart

What a waste to attempt to change behavior without truly
understanding the driving needs that cause such behavior!"
— Robert S. McGee, *The Search for Significance*[1]

O Lord, all my longing is before you;
my sighing is not hidden from you.
— Psalm 38:9

Like many teens that come to counseling, Marissa
had absolutely no interest in talking to me. Her
parents made the appointment after their youngest
daughter saw swear words carved on Marissa's fore-
arm and inner thigh. They were shocked by this dis-
covery. Never would they have imagined Marissa cutting herself.

Marissa rarely did anything unexpected. Compli-
ant and obedient, she seemed to be gliding through
adolescence. Although she was quiet and reserved,
her parents said she never seemed sad or depressed.
She appeared to have a very strong relationship with
God. She definitely preferred solitude to social activities, but occasionally, she would spend time with a
close friend or two.

From her parent's perspective, nothing in her life seemed to warrant such aberrant actions. Completely baffled by their daughter's behavior, Marissa's parents desperately wanted someone to help them figure out what could be going on deep within their daughter's heart that could possibly compel her to injure herself.

When I tried to talk to Marissa about the marks, she refused to acknowledge me. I could see teardrops trickling onto her jeans. But Marissa's heels were dug in. In fact, throughout our entire time together, she kept her long black hair draped over the right side of her face, completely concealing her expression. She respectfully listened but never acknowledged or responded to my comments and questions.

Knowing time was limited, I shared a bit about the power of each person's heart and its deep longing to be satisfied. I cautioned her by saying if we ignore our hearts and core desires that flow from them, we can unknowingly become overwhelmed or even controlled by the relentless yearnings that resound from this place within all of us.

More tears. More silence. I listed a few core desires that strive to control the heart during adolescence and young adulthood. I let her know these would increasingly beckon her to pay attention to them. In fact, she had already begun to search for something to quiet the ache. I finished by encouraging her to pay attention to her desires in order to learn how to manage them. Ignoring or dismissing them would only cause the emptiness to intensify, forcing her to heed their cries and respond.

Marissa appeared to be listening to every word. Even so, she never looked at me and never uttered a word. At the end of the session, she stood up and silently left my office. She missed her next appointment. Her parents explained that she refused to return, and they felt uncomfortable forcing her to come.

Not expecting to see Marissa ever again, I was surprised when her name reappeared on my schedule exactly one year later (almost to the date). This time it was at her request. And this time she had quite a bit to say. With a quiver in her voice and tears dripping down her cheeks, Marissa said she had been consumed with the little knowledge she had gained from me about her heart, its core desires, and the cries associated with each of them.

Because I couldn't fully remember what I had shared, I asked her to tell me what she remembered. Marissa listed a few of the eight core desires we will explore more fully in Section Two. She said she now recognized how her pain might be due to unmet longings. With a newfound wish to understand and care for her hidden heart, Marissa—along with her parents—committed to the counseling process.

What struck me then still strikes me today. For one whole year this timid and tattered fifteen-year-old girl reflected on words that offered her a reasonable explanation of how her inner state affected her outward actions. For one whole year she observed herself and others and validated what she'd learned. And then, after considering what she'd heard and personally experienced, she came back to gain more insight.

She and her parents were eager to know how she could better cope with the powerful desires that seemed to vie for control of her. In sessions and through a parent seminar, they learned why core desires suddenly demand so much attention during the adolescent years. They also gained a better understanding of why relationships with others, and especially with Christ, are critical for everyone as they deal with the desires of the heart.

Marissa's story provides just one portrait of an adolescent trying to understand and cope with the distress of her heart. Her behavior may look very different from the teens you know. However, the eight core desires that led Marissa to cutting as a coping strategy exist within the heart of every single teenager. Since so many teens (and adults) are unfamiliar with this central space we call the heart, they may be unaware of the core desires that dwell there.

When talking about the heart, younger teens often assume I'm referring to the actual organ in their ribcages. Even those who recognize the word's association with the innermost self typically don't know how to define or describe this place. I can't blame them. Our culture has muddied the meaning of the word. Pop songs portray the heart as an emotional and turbulent place within us. Popular clichés such as "Follow your heart," "Eat your heart out," and "Have a heart," cloud the picture even more.

No wonder teens seem befuddled by the concept of the heart. The heart can seem ambiguous. We talk about it but can't see it. Yet intense emotions that originate there are felt, making it hard to ignore. For most, the angst and agony coming from feeling empty or dissatisfied eventually motivates them to delve in, discover, and deal with their hidden hearts.

The Heart Defined

Since a word in context can often help clarify its meaning, exploring how the word *heart* is used in the Bible may enable us to come up with a coherent definition. The Hebrew word for heart is *leb* or *lebab* and the Greek word is *kardia*. Together, these words appear more than one thousand times throughout the Old and New Testaments.[2] Apart from referring to the actual organ, both the Greek and Hebrew texts use this word to refer to many different aspects of our being. There are four meanings, however, that tend to be most prevalent.[3]

First, the word heart refers to the *place of thought, reasoning, memory, and knowledge.* The verse, *But to this day the Lord has not given you a heart to understand or eyes to see or ears to hear,* describes the heart as a place of understanding and reason (Deut. 29:4). In the New

Testament, when Mary *treasured up all these things, pondering them in her heart,* we again see it described as a place where contemplation or reflection occurs. (Luke. 2:19) These verses demonstrate how the heart is connected to our mental or cognitive processes.

In the Bible, *emotions and sentiment* are also frequently linked with the word *heart.* Passages such as, *Let not your hearts be troubled* and *You have put more joy in my heart* capture the wide range of feelings experienced there (John. 14:1, Ps. 4:7). In this cavern in the soul lies the seat of grief, anger, overflowing love, and deep gratitude. Any and all emotions seem to travel through the heart.

Linked to both thoughts and feelings are *the acts of the will, intentions, or deeds.* This is a third common connection with the word *heart.* When Peter asked, *"Why is it that you have contrived this deed in your heart?"* he implied that within it, judgments or conclusions are formed (Acts 5:4). Similarly, when Paul says to the Corinthians, *Each one must do just as he has purposed in his heart,* he describes the heart as a place of resolution (2 Cor. 9:7, NASB). From these two passages we glean that the purpose behind behavior originates in the heart.

The last recurring meaning associates a person's *morality or conscience* with the heart. This usage implies that a person's overall character or virtue is tied to this portion of our being. For example, in Mark 7:21–22 when Jesus says, *"For from within, out of the heart of man, come evil thoughts, sexual immorality, theft, murder, adultery, coveting, wickedness, deceit, sensuality, envy, slander, pride, foolishness,"* he links immoral choices with the heart. This meaning seems to be used when the writer is referring to the root or central core of mankind.

These four descriptions capture distinct yet overlapping aspects of who we are. Collectively they create a rich and more meaningful definition of a word that can seem obscure. Putting these meanings within a circular diagram, we get a visual sense of the four primary parameters of the heart. Thus, for the purposes of this book, when we refer to the heart, we are referring to *a central, hidden place containing the thoughts, emotions, will, and morality of a person.*

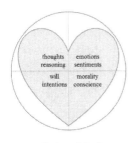

The heart defined

Diagram 1: The Heart Defined

Within the heart lie some of our most significant aspects. Each of these plays a powerful role in how we live. Not surprisingly, the heart is often considered the control center, or *springs of life* (Prov. 4:23

NASB). Everyone who wishes to rear a child *in the way he should go* (Prov. 22:6 NASB) eventually realizes that this task is impossible if the heart is ignored or overlooked.

Heart Core Desires

Now that we have a richer meaning of the word *heart*, we must consider how core desires relate to it. In the social and medical sciences, core desires are often termed emotional needs and are typically correlated with the social-emotional well-being of an individual. In the Bible core desires are repeatedly acknowledged and validated as coming from the heart (Job 17:11; Ps. 20:5, 21:2, 37:4).

In that central place four critical corners intersect. This intersection, or crossroads, is the point at which desires exist. This point of connection makes sense. A person's cravings, longings, or desires are tethered to their thoughts, emotions, will, and morality.

Using the previous definitions and the depiction of the hidden heart, we can now identify the eight core desires by the cry or exclamation associated with each one. These spring from that central crossroads of the heart since they are impacted by each of the four corners of our inner self.

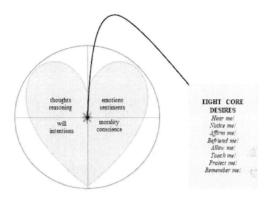

Diagram 2: Desires at Central Point of Intersection

Consider Marissa and my first session with her. Although she refused to speak, when I brought up the subject of desires in a general sense, her heart clearly began to stir. Her tears and eventual decision to return were evidence that she had made this connection between her heart, its core desires, and the cries associated with each of them.

While many innate longings spring from the heart, the eight that undeniably consume most teens tend to be core desires. Even though they may be unnamed or unrecognized by them or their families, core desires are repeatedly confirmed by verbal and behavioral expressions. In other words, look at what they say and do. The good, the bad, and the ugly often are attempts at satisfying a core desire. Both teens and the caring adults who regularly interact with them are significantly impacted by these desires.

For example, consider the teen that may be obsessed with making straight A's in school. If and when she receives a grade well below the one she'd hoped for, she feels anxiety. When she comes home from school, she shares her grade with Mom, secretly hoping she will ignore the grade and affirm her effort.

When her mom instead begins to question her studying habits, as well as the choices she made throughout the week, this bright young girl nods her head, listens to her mom's suggestions, and leaves the room. While her mother certainly did nothing wrong by offering her perspective, she completely missed the deeper source of her daughter's pain. Her daughter may learn in order to receive the affirmation her heart is craving—to be valued for herself alone—she must work harder and perform perfectly.

Core desires propel the expressed behavior. Just any perceived "want" differs from core desires. For example, a teen may want a first kiss, but the driver may be the core desire to be touched. Knowing the desire that leads to verbal or physical actions enables us to live a more authentic and wholehearted life.

Writer and theologian Frederick Buechner writes "that what we hunger for perhaps more than anything else is to be known in our full humanness, and yet that is often just what we also fear more than anything else."[4] Core desires are an extension of this deep desire and provide a means to being known. Deep inside everyone lies the unending desire to be heard, noticed, affirmed, befriended, allowed, touched, protected, and remembered.

These desires only grow stronger as kids enter adolescence and young adulthood and undergo major changes. These changes cause desires to intensify or even explode. How teens cope with core desires can and will, both positively and negatively, influence what they do and who they become.

I believe Sir Francis Bacon's oft quoted statement, "Knowledge is power." I repeatedly see teens become both empowered and relieved once they realize how core desires regularly affect their thoughts, feelings, actions, and moral inclinations. Deliberate, matter-of-fact conversations about core desires can explain so much of what's going on in and around adolescence. This information initially helped Marissa begin her personal journey of awareness. She was able to validate and affirm their existence as forces within her.

Knowing and naming core desires and discovering where they come from is just the beginning for a teen. Knowing why they continually affect their actions and why the body actually aches when they are not met is the next step. In order to understand more fully, Marissa and her family had to grasp how the heart related to the rest of her soul. We'll explore this connection in the next chapter.

Chapter 2

Heart in Soul: The Outer and Inner Self

A soul without a center feels constantly
vulnerable to people or circumstances.
— John Ortberg, *Soul Keeping*[1]

As a deer pants for flowing streams,
so pants my soul for you, O God.
My soul thirsts for God,
for the living God.
— Psalm 42:1–2

As a kid I was designated "the navigator"—holder of the maps—on family trips. Neither my sisters (nor my mom) ever vied for my title, but I always felt privileged to get the job. Before every trip my dad and I would unfold the large paper map and locate our starting and ending points. Then we would consider all possible routes and decide on the best one. When we were done, I always lingered a bit longer over the map. I wanted to know what lay beyond what we could see while on our journey.

Soul: Outer and Inner Self

Although we can't map the heart as we've defined it, a diagram along with a metaphor can help us grasp the impact of heart desires on the soul. "The soul is that aspect of your whole being that correlates, integrates, and enlivens everything going on in the various dimensions of the self."[2] These dimensions can be grouped as the outer self and the inner self.

To illustrate this concept, imagine a circle to represent a person's soul. Within this circle lie four concentric circles that radiate from the center. While the soul is far greater than the sum of these parts, these pieces are central to who we are as human beings.

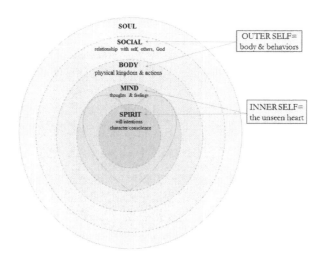

Diagram 3: The Heart in the Soul (adapted from
Dallas Willard's model of the soul)

The social and body layers of the soul together make up what the ESV translation describes as the "outer self" (2 Cor. 4:16). As mortal beings, these layers inevitably deteriorate or decay over time. Starting with the outermost layer, the soul contains the *social* dimension. The social extends beyond our relationships with other people; it includes our relationship with ourselves and with God. Since most social interactions can be seen, this layer is considered external.

For example, when your teen finds out that a close friend shared something embarrassing about her with others, you can observe her choices, reactions, and the way she relates to you or others. Whether she withdraws, acts dramatically or irritably, or writes bitter posts on social media, her outward behaviors represent the social portion of her soul.

Moving inward to the next layer is the *body*. Dallas Willard, the author from whom I adapted this diagram, describes the body as "our primary energy source or 'strength'—our personalized 'power pack.'"[3] With our bodies we move and interact with the world. While this circle certainly includes physical organs, limbs, and physical sensations, it encompasses far more than that. Although others can't see our organs and sensations, our physical bodies and actions can be seen. Thus, this layer is also external.

When the same teen grits her teeth, cries, paces around in her room, complains of a headache, and collapses in her bed from physical and emotional exhaustion, this behavior describes the bodily aspect of her soul coping with the stressor.

The "inner self" consists of the mind and the spirit. The *mind,* comprised of both thoughts and feelings, is the home of reason, ideas, images, perception, imagination, and revelation. Because all of these are colored with an emotion or tone, feelings and sentiments are also in the mind. The two are intimately intertwined and inseparable from each other. Even though we can gain clues about a person's thoughts or feelings, apart from God, only the individual knows what fills his mind (1 Cor. 2:11). Consequently, the content of the mind is hidden and depends on words and/or actions to reveal what is there.

The innermost layer is the *spirit.* Although this aspect of the soul intimately guides our lives, it's difficult to fully comprehend. Here lie the intentions, motives, and even moral conscience of a person. For the believer, this is the space where God's Spirit begins its transformation. Sanctification—the process of becoming holy—occurs as the Holy Spirit influences or forms the other dimensions of the soul. Although this area is undoubtedly the most hidden, we know from experience that in this space, we find both great strength and overwhelming weakness.

These internal dimensions of the soul together make up the "inner being" (Eph. 3:16). Since the mind and spirit represent the four most common biblical usages of the word *heart* (see Diagram 1), in this book I will equate the inner being with the heart. For this reason, I have added the faint outline of a heart to the center of Diagram 3 to demonstrate how it encompasses both the mind and the spirit.

Comparing this circle diagram to a trampoline, we can say that movement in one area always resonates to other areas within and across the concentric circles. In short, each part of the soul automatically influences and is influenced by the other parts. Distress in the social or bodily dimensions (outer self) influences the state of the heart (inner self). The opposite is true, as well. When the heart has a measure of angst or anguish, whether we are aware of it or not, the physical body and social relationships are affected at some level. The intensity of the disruptions in any part affects the reverberations felt across the soul.

Development Provokes Core Desires

I often tell parents and teens that no one can force a teen to pay attention to these disruptions. However, as life unfolds, they repeatedly give them opportunities to figure out what is occurring at their core. The most intrusive disruptions relate to their physical, social, emotional, and cognitive development. As changes begin to happen, the discomfort and distress adolescents experience offer them the opportunity to acknowledge their hidden hearts. Hopefully, they seek the Creator of their hearts to fully satisfy their deepest longings.

Could it be that our loving and merciful God allows so many aspects of teen development to shift at the same time in order for adolescents to pay attention to the innermost parts of themselves? C.S. Lewis wrote, "Pain insists upon being attended to. God whispers to us in our pleasures, speaks in our consciences, but shouts in our pains. It is his megaphone to rouse a deaf world."[3] Pain wakes us up and forces us to recognize what we really desire.

Adults know that pain and puberty go hand in hand. Whether social, physical, or emotional pain, God uses massive changes occurring in the outer layers of the soul to agitate, unsettle, and awaken the inner layers of the soul. It shouldn't surprise us then when core desires begin to explode from the heart or when repeated changes relentlessly rock an adolescent's world.

We observed a bit of this unfold the year our youngest son turned 13 years old. From infancy, Sam never stopped humming or singing. Random remarks would lead him to warble a portion of a TV jingle, a theme song from a movie, or a pop tune from the radio. By the time he was twelve years old, singing, strumming his guitar, and plunking piano keys was a major pastime. Sam was a happy kid who found joy, comfort, and plenty of affirmation from others through music.

One day when he sang, instead of the high notes he easily produced, a scratchy-squeaky noise came out of his mouth. His initial amusement quickly changed to deep frustration and embarrassment. Even though Sam knew his voice would change, he wasn't prepared for the time it took to stabilize. To deal with it, he constantly moaned and complained. "My stupid voice is ruining my life," he'd say again and again. Our happy go lucky kid was temporarily replaced by a sullen, negative, restless, and even fearful teen.

While we knew this mixed bag of emotions was likely a result of many changes, Sam feared he would never be able to sing well again. This slight change in his body rattled other segments of his soul, as well. His **social** interactions changed. Any comment or observation about his voice or any other physical change caused him to become defensive and edgy. For a while he was too self-conscious to spend time with friends who were musically inclined.

Sam's **mind** was also affected. While his conversation wasn't always about his voice, this small shift in development awakened him to the unpredictability of life. Even though Sam had a relationship with God, his **spirit** was clearly rattled. Many questions about God, His plan, His goodness, His mercy, His presence, and other aspects of His character regularly surfaced.

Although a voice change is fairly insignificant, it offers a vivid example of how a slight disruption can unsettle every part of the soul. If this change can bring about such disharmony in a relatively happy kid, then consider what adolescents endure when so much shifts simultaneously.

Since we are made in God's image, our souls crave peace and wholeness even if we won't fully experience them on this side of heaven. Thus, as discord and disruptions occur, every segment of the soul is subjected to increasing distress. Because so many changes unfold as teens enter puberty, the physical aspects of the soul specifically experience monumental disruptions.

Sudden growth spurts, a facial makeover, and awkward sexual changes lead to a more mature, adult frame. A hidden yet significant portion of the bodily changes occurs in the brain. Here, a critical reconstruction is underway so that more sophisticated cognitive abilities allow teens to perceive and engage with others in a whole new way.

On top of these bodily changes are the social-emotional and psychological shifts that take place. As teens spend increasingly more time with peers, they learn to become more self-aware and socially aware, all while they experience emotional highs and lows. These encounters are critical since they play a huge role in helping them detach and form their own identities.

In the following diagram, I included these intrusions caused by adolescent development in their correlating segments of the soul. Within the outer rings, labeled **SOCIAL** and **BODY,** lie the four primary areas of adolescent development—physical, cognitive, social-emotional, and psychological. The **MIND** and **SPIRIT** segments, which together comprise the inner self, are now depicted side by side inside the heart since together they encapsulate the broad meaning of the word *heart*. We can now see how ongoing changes in development easily provoke the heart. Likewise, the emptiness or abundance of this inner place can rattle the ongoing fluctuations taking place in the outer layers.

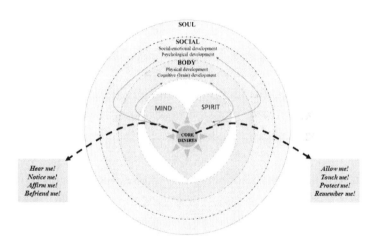

Diagram 4: Developmental Disruptions Impact Emerging Desires

In my work with teens, I regularly get to see the reciprocal relationship between the inner and outer dimensions of the soul. When kids seem to make steady progress as developmental changes unfold, heart needs are more likely satisfied in a healthy manner. And, as these longings continue to be satisfied, the four aspects of development benefit, as well. Conversely, when kids are stuck or regressing in any one area of development, heart needs almost always intensify. The longer the emptiness or angst from core desires continues, the more it exacerbates developmental problems.

A teen's inherent need to be heard, noticed, affirmed, befriended, allowed, touched, protected, and remembered matters a great deal. The healthy satisfaction of these desires almost always results in the forward progression of each area of development.

The obvious relationship between adolescent development and the desires of the heart certainly does not surprise God. He formed their innermost parts and knit them together (Ps. 139:13). He lovingly orchestrates these unfolding changes. His purpose is to use the disorientation, distress, and disappointment to compel them to tune into their restless, hidden hearts prior to adulthood.

While these relentless desires can be difficult to understand, and even more difficult to manage, they need to be addressed. The enemy of the heart is determined to keep you and your teen from ever recognizing or validating them. He prefers that we remain confused by what is seen and experienced and dismiss any connection between the inner and outer layers of the soul. "Quench the heart," he says when challenges arise. "When you feel that nagging ache, grab something, anything, to numb it or distract you. Better yet, dismiss your heart altogether and pretend there's no ache at all."

Parents and caring adults can help teens understand how these parts of the soul relate to one another. Using teens' own experiences, adults can affirm, offer guidance, and give insight into God's greater purposes for instilling the core desires in their hearts. We need not wait for conflict or pain in a teen's life to bring up the subject of the heart. In fact, since so much is going on in the outer layers of the soul, heart crises can often be a much more difficult time to address it. Instead of waiting for a crisis, we must be more intentional about bringing up the core desires that emerge so powerfully day after day in the lives of our adolescent children.

Our God, who cares deeply about the heart—the inner self—knows that in order for us to become fully alive adults, the heart and the desires that reside therein require ongoing attention. Consider this: if Christian parents only talk about God when there is pain, they miss out on many opportunities to connect everyday experiences with Him. As we will see in the next chapter, the many changes associated with adolescent development have a very special way of urging our kids to tune in to this inner space. Then they can begin to live the lives for which they were created.

Chapter 3

Heartstrings: The Outer Self

Adolescence is just one big walking pimple.
— Carol Burnett[1]

Be gracious to me, O Lord, for I am in distress;
my eye is wasted from grief;
my soul and my body also.
— Psalm 31:9

The minute I closed my office door, she collapsed on the couch and sobbed uncontrollably. "I hate my face. I hate my body. I have no friends. And I am so mad at myself for caring at all!" For the first time in many sessions together, Madeline showed emotion.

I learned that earlier in the day, she had searched her closet to find warmer clothes. When the search led her to realize that last year's clothes no longer fit, a mountain of emotions spilled out. Although she knew she had grown and her parents would happily buy her new clothes, this dilemma allowed other discomforting feelings to come to the surface. Her dilemma wasn't just her physical change in size or feeling different or alone. It was everything all at once and her inability to manage or keep it contained. She felt utterly helpless.

Madeline's distress demonstrates how a lot of little changes have a way of piling up and pushing out the stuff simmering at the center of the soul. In the last chapter, I likened the four primary areas of adolescent development—physical, cognitive, social-emotional, and psychological—to the outer layers of the soul. In this chapter we will gain a basic understanding of how the outer self can easily derail a teen. I have provided two common reactions that tend to be associated with each layer of change. These reactions can be likened to heartstrings that tug at the core desires, causing them to emerge.

The BODY: Physical Transformations

Physical changes are the first characteristics most people associate with adolescence. A massive increase in hormones triggers these inward and outward bodily changes. While the timing of these changes varies from person to person, in general, females enter puberty before males. Significant growth in primary sex characteristics typically indicates that the process has begun.

Females notice the appearance of breast buds as well as the presence of a mucus-like discharge from the vagina that occurs from the thickening of the uterus wall. For males, the primary outward indicators include the enlargement of the penis, testes, and prostate gland.

These early markers are soon followed by changes in secondary sex characteristics such as steady weight gain, growth spurts, and changes in hair texture as well as the presence of pubic and underarm hair. Along the way, females will have their first menstrual period (menses) and males their first ejaculation (spermarche).

Facial changes also begin to unfold as the skin thickens. Acne often appears, and both the jaw and nose grow larger. Until these changes are complete, an adolescent's face may appear rather disproportionate. For males, facial changes are accompanied by changes in their voices. Lower pitched, deeper sounds evolve as both their pharynx and larynx significantly lengthen.

All of these changes happen within just a two to five-year time frame. No wonder few if any people desire a return to this era of major physical transformations. Even one of these changes requires an adjustment. Research confirms that one of the biggest hurdles has to do with *when* these changes begin to happen. The onset of puberty impacts males and females very differently.

Girls who enter puberty earlier than their peers are at greater risk for social and/or emotional difficulties. Thus, they experience higher rates of anxiety and depression.[2] For girls, adjusting to larger hips, thighs, fuller breasts, weight gain, and increased attention can be tough in a sexualized culture that venerates both a curvy, yet slim figure. A girl's inability to fully control the timing or outcome of her body growth may lead some to cope in unhealthy ways—crash dieting, food restrictions, over exercising, or using clothing to disguise her figure or alternatively dressing in a way that flaunts it.

For males, most of the physical changes are seen as desirable. A taller, broader, stronger, faster, and deeper sounding male is perceived as more capable—athletically as well as socially and academically. Males who appear less developed may be mocked, criticized, bullied, or excluded from certain groups. Like girls, teen guys cope in different ways— intensifying workouts, altering their diets to increase muscle mass and weight, or attempting to distract themselves or others from delayed development by excelling in social, academic, or extracurricular activities.

As I mentioned earlier, two common reactions tend to be associated with each layer of change. Throughout the physical evolution, expect to see adolescents **comparing and contrasting** themselves with their former selves and with others. These actions naturally begin as teens notice their rapidly changing physical bodies and that of their peers. As they adjust to their new frames, they ask, *what do I/they think of me/them? Am I beautiful, handsome? Will someone choose me?* Questions like these arouse the whole spectrum of emotions—from fear to frenzy and contempt to contentment.

Regardless of whether teens ever share thoughts or feelings, as long as they privately or openly compare and contrast themselves with others, certain core desires intensify. These propel them to seek people who will listen to them, notice them, affirm them, befriend them, allow them to make a contribution, touch them, protect them, and offer safety as they adjust to this huge disruption in their lives.

The BODY: Cognitive Renovation

Although we can actually see most of the physical transformations taking place in the pubescent teen, the most impactful change in the body actually occurs in the brain. Until recently, we assumed the human brain was fully mature well before adolescence. Thanks to an explosion in neuroscience research, we now know that prior to adolescence, brain cells (neurons) create millions of connections (neural pathways) as kids learn, grow, and interact with people and the world around them. The massive expansion of these pathways across the brain and body during childhood and adolescence is called "proliferation."

Once a child enters the teen years, neural pathways continue forming, but another process begins to unfold. In order to become faster and more efficient, the brain needs to clip or prune what is not used. Think of the many neural pathways in the brain as a drawer overstuffed with cables from the many electronic devices you've purchased over the years. Every time you open the drawer, you have to find and separate the cable you want from those you rarely use. Once it is untangled, you mash the others back into the drawer. Mentally, you tell yourself that at some point you should probably throw out those you no longer need.

This analogy illustrates why pruning occurs. By pruning pathways, the brain is getting rid of connections that are rarely used. Then it protects and reinforces those that are still utilized. This whole process (myelinating) starts in the back of the brain during early adolescence and ends at the front of the brain (prefrontal cortex) at around 25 years of age.

Because of the massive changes in the brain, the adolescent years should be viewed as both a window of opportunity and a window of vulnerability. The habits, beliefs, perceptions, knowledge, skills, and other patterns of behaviors that are acquired during this time become wired and protected in the brain, making it part of the hardware. We affirm this process when we consider helpful, hopeful, or healthy behaviors that now become easily accessible or reflexive. If these are destructive or unhelpful, however, the damage to the brain, body, or relationships could be lasting since protected pathways are more difficult to eliminate once pruning is completed.

While we can't see the massive renovation of the brain, visible cognitive shifts prove the brain is growing and developing. Teens can marshal facts more speedily (especially in arguments) and utilize logic and deductive reasoning. Their language skills improve as pruning allows them to more readily access words and thoughts. The rational regions of the brain (cortex), though still easily sabotaged by the emotional (limbic) brain, slowly offer them the ability to manage their emotions better, address problems, and deal with stressors. Because the brain is making major changes, adolescents are deeply reflective, sharp yet critical, or sullen and emotionally vulnerable—all in one day.

As cognitive abilities expand and refine, adolescents have the capacity to become even more aware of the deepest segments of the soul. Like a meter on a car, teens can now intuit whether they are empty or full, content or wanting, full of angst or ecstasy, and in distress or at peace. They may not always find the words, but many are aware of the internal unrest they experience when core desires are lacking.

Because of this major brain renovation, expect to see teens *examining* and *expressing* themselves more over the course of adolescence. Sometimes, a seemingly nosy or mouthy teen may be actively investigating and reflecting on the world and people around them. Even if their pursuit of knowledge or their thoughts about what they observe seem annoying, their maturing brains enable them to consider everything in a whole new way.

As you can imagine, this aspect of development, and the actions associated with it, tug at most, if not all, of the eight core desires. Ever hear a teen say, "No one ever listens to me"? Or, "You always criticize my opinions!" The brain thrives in relationships and suffers in isolation. As adolescents search for people to gratify desires, synaptic connections (learning) occur through painful and/or pleasurable encounters with others.

The Social Segment: Social-Emotional Changes

Since healthy brain development requires social interactions, we shouldn't be surprised that major social-emotional shifts happen simultaneously. The depth and breadth of a teen's relationships with others slowly expand. These often begin with primarily same sex peer groups during early adolescence and move to a more mixed group of intimate connections with individuals of the same or opposite sex. These social encounters give adolescents the opportunity to become more self-aware, self-regulated, socially aware, and relational. Together, these represent the four pillars of social-emotional development.

Self-awareness is the ability to know what you think, feel, and desire. More time spent with others offers teens more opportunities to become self-aware. Disagreements, as dramatic or petty as they can be, also help them become aware of emotions such as anger, excitement, fear, anxiety, or hurt. They also discover how they are triggered.

Through social encounters and the conflict that always ensues, adolescents slowly learn how to *self-regulate*. They can both monitor and manage their emotions as they ebb and flow. Even though an increase in hormones often intensifies felt emotions, a better brain gives them the ability to slow down their reactions by considering consequences, thinking more rationally, and finding language to express their thoughts and requests. Without basic self-regulation skills, adolescents find it hard to cultivate friendships.

Another pillar of social-emotional development is *social awareness*—empathizing with another person. Using verbal and non-verbal cues, socially aware kids can tune in to the body language and facial cues of an individual or group. Research demonstrates this ability develops slowly since younger adolescents rely more on the emotional centers of the brain to process these cues instead of a more advanced cortex.[3]

The fourth pillar is *relational*. Teens should experience increased interactions with people in different settings to help them develop relationally. Conversations, conflict, heartfelt exchanges, group gatherings, athletics, extracurricular activities, part-time work, or any social interaction requires their brains to improve their connections with others. The *relational* pillar becomes evident as an adolescent's ability to connect, communicate, cooperate, and resolve conflict with others improves over time.

With respect to social-emotional development, the two actions that tug at heart core desires are **connect-**

ing and conflicting. In their attempts to create more connections, clashes with peers, parents, and others occur. Although certainly taxing (especially for those who get pulled in!), these difficulties allow teens to realize how much they need relationships to help them satisfy the longings of the hidden heart. They begin to understand how disconnecting with others negatively impacts the state of their hearts. Conversely, when teens work hard to maintain their relationships with a variety of people, the inner layers of the soul tend to reap the peace that is sown.

The Social Segment: Psychological Changes

Social-emotional changes, along with physical and cognitive shifts, allow adolescents to begin thinking about their identities. More than ever, they begin to reflect upon the questions "Who am I?" and "Who do I want to be?" Their pursuit of answers helps them become a separated and individuated human being. This process of detaching and defining oneself apart from others is the primary task or feature of psychological development.

By spending more time away from primary caregivers, adolescents begin to incorporate the knowledge, beliefs, habits, and skills they gain from outside experiences. They combine them with what they choose to assimilate from their childhood years. Done well, this formation of a new self is a slow, messy process that depends upon increased freedom, exposure to people and experiences, courage, and risk taking. During this process, back and forth movement occurs between two worlds—the familiar (home) and the unfamiliar (away from home).

Like a toddler playing dress up, adolescents try on and temporarily adopt the styles, beliefs, attitudes, and/or actions of others. They are figuring out what to integrate into their new identities. Parental permission, as well as personal permission, plays a role in deciding what sticks. Along the way, they hold on to or release pieces of the past and present in order to slowly become their own persons.

Many contradictory feelings are associated with this aspect of development. Adolescents will feel fearful, insecure, restless, and worried while also feeling free, excited, empowered, and delighted. And shouldn't this be expected? They are stepping away from all they have known and moving toward a world of possibilities that will play a huge role in determining who they become.

Teens who are protected or prohibited from being able to separate and individuate often lack the inner core or emotional strength formed by this psychological process. Conversely, those who have no boundaries as they step beyond home are likely to experience serious and even unfortunate consequences. These interfere with their ability to safely individuate. Finding a balance between the two extremes explains why this season can be particularly challenging for parents, as well as their teens.

Throughout psychological development, the two actions that often provoke core desires are **testing and taking off**. Repeatedly, I see adolescents unknowingly engage in behaviors that seem to test their connections with their primary caregivers. Before they begin to separate, they inherently need to know if their caregivers are secure and anchored as individuals. Similar to a boat testing an anchor, they slowly let the rope grow longer. As they begin to take off, they test the principles, practices, beliefs, assumptions, and values they've been taught to see how they stand up and compare to what they discover beyond the borders.

These actions may appear rebellious, but teens need a measure of healthy rebellion to detach and define who they are apart from their moms or dads. Along the way, adolescents look for people who will satisfy their core desires. These desires are repeatedly aroused as they test and take off from what they know to discover who they will become.

Looking Ahead

We have reviewed how developmental disruptions cause a disintegration of sorts within and between the segments of the teen's soul. Now we can better understand why core desires take center stage during this season of life. To the extent that longings are satisfied in a healthy manner, adolescent development benefits. When core desires are deprived or ignored, teens may experience delays in certain areas of development.

This relationship between core desires and an adolescent's development both progresses and regresses. Every teen must be helped to recognize and respond to unmet core desires. Some of their best and worst decisions will be prompted by these longings.

For this reason, I believe parents and caring adults should take time to understand each of the eight core desires and how they impact the attitudes and actions of every adolescent. Doing so will open your eyes to the many opportunities you have to lovingly direct your teens toward Christ and community in order to satisfy their hearts' core desires.

Section Two
Heart Core Desires:
The "Inner Self"

In this section I will describe the eight heart cries of teens in greater detail. Each chapter begins with a brief portrait of a teen's attempt to satisfy one of the desires. While I've changed the names and identifying details to protect the privacy of individuals, these very different accounts give us a more vivid picture of how these "great eight" compel our kids to act in ways that range from very destructive to very God honoring.

Each chapter is divided into three key sections: *RECOGNIZE the Cry, RESPOND in a Helpful Way, and RELAY Critical Truths.* The *RECOGNIZE* section identifies typical methods kids use to satisfy each desire. The *RESPOND* segment gives beneficial ways for parents and caring adults to react to these longings. Finally, the *RELAY* portion offers two truths that we can share. Each reflects God's response to their heart cries and their unending need for relationship.

God fills us with His Spirit and gives us the capacity to offer others a taste of Him. We can't be continual rainspouts perpetually quenching teens' thirsty hearts. By sharing the Creator's promises to satisfy their thirsts in a relationship with Him, many kids will be spurred to run toward—instead of away from—the Father. I believe that recognizing, responding, and relaying truths about the eight heart cries will transform your relationship with your teen.

Chapter 4

"Hear me." I long to be heard and understood.

I feel like I'm at the bottom of a well. I feel like I'm way down this deep, deep hole and I'm looking up and all there is this little dot of light and I have to shout at the top of my lungs for anyone to hear me and even when I do, I say the wrong thing or they don't really listen or they're just humouring me.
— Patrick Ness, *The Rest of Us Just Live Here*[1]

You have searched me, Lord,
and you know me.
You know when I sit and when I rise;
you perceive my thoughts from afar.
You discern my going out and my lying down;
you are familiar with all my ways.
— Psalm 139: 1–3 NIV

"I know exactly what to do to make them listen to me," boasted 17-year-old Stephen. "When I'm crazy and reckless, my parents pay attention to me." And that's exactly what he did. When I met him, he was drinking, using drugs, sneaking out at night, and skipping school.

Unfortunately, his plan didn't work. The more Stephen did, the less his parents cared to listen to what lay beneath his behavior. Stephen's aggressive stance with them made it tough for them to get close to his heart. Their inability to hear and understand what was really going on beneath the façade led him to engage in even more unruly behaviors.

Stephen really didn't want to live life so recklessly, but at this point, he knew no other way to deal with his feelings. He'd been adopted at birth by a mom and dad with one biological child. Although he knew he was loved, he always felt so different from his family. Not knowing anyone else who was adopted, he felt set apart—and even inferior—compared to his peers.

While he desperately wanted to know where he came from, he didn't know how to start the conversation. In his mind, exposing his deepest vulnerabilities was closely tied to inferiority. Not surprisingly, trapped feelings converted into disruptive behaviors that sadly pushed potential listeners away. His actions did, however, get people's attention.

Because we are made in the image of God—THE Great Communicator—we are born with this core desire to be known. As our kids develop and move through the dramatic, yet disruptive growth processes central to adolescence, the "Hear me!" cry will only intensify. In order to be genuinely known by others, teens must be willing and able to communicate.

When I introduce core desires to adolescents, I often ask them to circle the two that they desire more than anything else—the ones that might compel them to do whatever it takes to satisfy the urge. More often than not, "Hear me" is one of the two. It certainly was for Stephen. Because core desires always impact the mind, body, and behavior, we can always find evidence of the cry if we look carefully.

RECOGNIZE the Cry

Whether kids are screaming, yelling, truant, shoplifting, being verbally or physically aggressive, addicted, overly engaged in social media, excessively sleeping, harming themselves, restricting food intake, over-exercising, suicidal, extremely withdrawn, overly social, or even sexually promiscuous, a message always lies beneath what is seen. Furthermore, adolescents who are unable to express themselves or who can't find people who will tune in to their deepest needs often use unruly or inappropriate behaviors to get their messages across. Why? Every kid, every teen, every adult greatly desires to be heard and understood.

Although most kids will attempt to use spoken words to express themselves, some can't. Others won't for fear of being derided or disregarded. As a result, they'll often try to communicate through immature and annoying strategies. They hope you'll take note. Remember that a kid who does nothing to be heard is either giving up on a relationship with you or believing that communicating matters of the heart are unnecessary or undesirable aspects of a relationship. Below, I list a few things they will do to be heard. If you see these in your home, your kid may be trying to tell you something.

Increased volume (shouting, crying, making noise, etc.)
"You never listen to me!"
"Nobody cares what I think!"

These pronouncements come from both kids and parents. A parent wants his request, the expectation, or the consequence to be heard. A kid wishes the parent would just stop and listen to his perspective. I call this song and dance "loud and louder." If yelling is how you learn to communicate when you really want people to tune in, both parent and child will turn up the volume a notch so the other will listen.

Sometimes, yelling has more to do with self-protection. Despite our God-given desire to be known, exposing thoughts and feelings is a vulnerable and discomforting experience. For the child who has been physically or emotionally wounded, shouting and verbal attacks can certainly keep people at a distance. Sadly, if she realizes that no one really knows the under layers of her heart, the pain and emptiness just grow deeper, and the longing to be heard intensifies.

Decreased volume (quiet, withdrawn, sullen)
C.S. Lewis once wrote, "I have learned now that while those who speak about one's miseries usually hurt, those who keep silence hurt more."[2] Although

it may be incredibly taxing to raise a loud and overly expressive child, it usually pales in comparison to the kid whose message is barely detectable and tough to decipher. Often, these kids are trying to compensate for the sibling whose chronic behavioral challenges keep them in the spotlight.

When obstacles come, instead of voicing their pain, they may withdraw, put on a smile, or try to live under the radar. Their hearts' desires are overlooked, overshadowed, and overruled. While they desire to be known, the idea of someone pursuing them feels uncomfortable. They discount their silence or retreat. Even introverted, shy kids need to learn to convey the content of their hearts with someone who cares.

Social media and technology

When I first began working with adolescents, I assumed *talking* meant speaking out loud. I also assumed the person with whom they were speaking was physically present (or at the very least on the phone with them). Now, if a kid is *talking*, she may actually be texting, messaging, Skyping, or even dating.

Through digital technology and social media, finding others who will listen to you has gotten much easier. Wherever they are, you can just dial up a friend in a chat room, message them through social media, or post your deepest darkest thoughts for the entire world to read.

The problem is that without a face in front of you, communicating your heart solely through digital means never quite satisfies. I recently met with a kid who adamantly defended her online friendship to her parents, who had expressed concern about how much time she spent chatting with her. Frustrated by the thought of being disconnected, she exclaimed, "If she is the only one who will listen to me, then of course I want to talk with her all the time!" That was the problem. She had no one else. Because she leaned so heavily on this relationship, she didn't have the energy to find other outlets.

Finding people who will respond through texts or online messages makes perfect sense to teens who don't feel anyone cares to hear them—even if they barely know them. While I will avoid making a blanket statement about whether *talking* through digital means is beneficial or detrimental, we must remember that it derives from the great need to be heard, to have someone wholeheartedly listen while you share whatever is on your heart.

Atypical behaviors
When words can't be found, aren't heard, or continue to be misunderstood, many adolescents will resort to immature and often reckless behaviors such as stomping, huffing, moaning, wailing—even collapsing. Others are slamming doors, stomping up the stairs, throwing a temper-tantrum, self-harming, running away, destroying property, and attacking. I can't think of a kid whose destructive, rebellious, or radical behavior wasn't in some way a desperate attempt to

cope and communicate. Anything illegal or out of the ordinary for your kid may be a way of nonverbally communicating that he needs to feel heard and understood.

Creative outlets

On the way home from my daughter's daily ballet class, she was always far more expressive than she was on the way there. After hearing and moving to the melody and the flow and rhythm of music, this quiet and shy girl was able to talk about tender areas of her heart that were often quite difficult for her to access.

Journals. Books. Music. Poems. Art. Theatre. Dance. Yes, even tattoos. Creative expressions like these can provide an avenue for adolescents to find their voices, regardless of whether they're the author, performer, participant, or spectator. Similar to a megaphone, these outlets bravely exclaim what a kid would never say outright. They can also be a welcomed avenue for kids to get a multi-layered message across to the world. Often, these actually help adolescents figure out what they're really thinking and feeling.

These are just a few of the ways our kids will communicate when they don't feel heard and understood. If you aren't seeing any of these behaviors, your teens are most likely relying on words to share their hearts. Whether their methods are harmful or helpful, the ball lies in your court to acknowledge and attend to the cry. After you recognize attempts to be heard, you'll eventually have the opportunity to respond. Hopefully, the way you do so will help them learn other appropriate and God-honoring ways to express themselves.

RESPOND in a Helpful Way

When a person genuinely and lovingly listens to another human being, he or she reflects Christ to the other. Through our relationships with kids, we have the power to shape their understanding of unconditional love, fatherhood, authority, grace, and mercy. In a world of people who wear masks and build impenetrable walls of self-protection, adolescents need people who will pursue their hearts while opening their own hearts.

Instead of fears, doubts, or fleshly reflexes, invite God's Spirit to flow through you. He'll give you the ability to really hear what teens are trying to say to you in word or deed. Don't ever assume you already know. Instead, cover your mouth, put down your defenses, and engage them in conversations. Here are other suggestions to help you stay tuned in, grounded, and responsive to the cries of your adolescent's heart.

Resist the temptation to disconnect.

Rarely are the words and tone of an adolescent polished, appropriate, or respectful. Although you must establish reasonable ground rules, when conversations get heated, the enemy wants more than anything for you to disengage. He hopes you'll push them away or walk away so you'll miss out on knowing what lies beneath their actions.

Instead of leaving, tell your kids what you need. If you need a break to take a deep breath, then set a time to reconvene. As you temporarily withdraw, consider what you have heard and what their intense reactions may reveal. Quite often, their emotional state, the direction of their gazes, the tears in their eyes, and the movement of their bodies are conveying what words can't. Because fear has a way of squelching vulnerability, when you stick around and project a genuine desire to hear their hearts, your teens are far more likely to share.

Ask more. Talk less.

Over three hundred questions were asked by Jesus and recorded in the gospels. He knew that good questions could often reveal the heart of the matter. Reflect His method by asking open-ended questions that can't be quickly answered with a *yes* or *no* response. Broad questions such as "What do you need from me right now?" or "What are you trying to tell me?" or "What is occupying a lot of brain space these days?" or "What was a high or low moment today/ this week?" may help get the conversation going.

Listen for emotional words and phrases that reveal their beliefs or viewpoints of themselves, you, others, or God. Use what you learned to formulate more probing questions. If they're not accustomed to your interest in them, try conversation toward the end of their day, when most adolescents admit they are more open to a parent's pursuit. Though you may be exhausted, parents and kids say that some of their best conversations occur late in the evening. Perhaps your fatigue will help you talk less and ask more.

Temper your emotions.

Kids often tell me they don't share some things with their parents because they fear the emotional beating or lecture they might receive." If we really want to parent them through their fears, frustrations, and fantasies, then we must project safety. Often, a parent must voice their concerns or fears. However, a harsh tone, heightened volume, or shaming posture will never invite a kid to hear your heart. Resist the temptation to defend your behavior or criticize their perspective with a tone of condemnation.

Own and confess your imperfections.

Our kids learn how to talk openly about hard, awkward, sensitive, difficult, private, and uncomfortable subject matter by the way we do the same. If we don't talk candidly and courageously with them, then we can't expect them to do so with us. We don't need to share personal and irrelevant "junk" with them. Nor do we need to filter all of our conversations. In the context of daily interactions, we can choose to talk about our thoughts and feelings about life, each other, work, family, God and so on.

Openness highlights a willingness to reveal imperfections as well as insights. They need to hear us admit our faults and ask for forgiveness—not just with them but with others as well. The way we express ourselves to others and to God will be one of the biggest predictors of how they'll choose to satisfy this desire in their own lives.

When heated conversations and conflict cause you to wound your child, humbly return to them and confess your sin. Confession is the first step in rebuilding a broken relationship. With expressions of regret and sorrow, model vulnerability by saying, "I messed up. Please forgive me for hurting you." Most of all, confession reminds them that you love them. You're genuinely interested in continuing the conversation.

Prompt conversation during ordinary events.
Parents repeatedly tell me that random and unplanned exchanges throughout the week tend to yield deeper conversations with their teens. While special time can still prompt healthy exchanges, many teens admit that a date or outing with a parent makes them feel under the spotlight, sometimes making it more awkward to be vulnerable.

Because facial expressions often confuse or even threaten a kid, sitting side by side instead of face-to-face may lead to deeper and more meaningful dialogues. The distraction of a task can also be just enough to drop a kid's protective shield to let you in.

Shift out of problem-solving mode.

Seeing an adolescent in pain can cause many parents to meld into fix-it mode. Because you don't own most of your adolescent's problems, you're not charged with solving them. In fact, many kids tell me they don't want their parents to mend or take charge of a solution. Instead, they want them to hear their pain and offer their presence, comfort, and hope.

God can use their difficulties to teach them a great deal about themselves, others, and this fallen world we live in. When we rescue them or try to relieve their discomfort, we teach them to fear pain instead of seeing it as an opportunity to be refined and strengthened. We also teach other-dependence rather than self-reliance. We don't withhold wisdom but then neither do we lead with it. Instead, as listeners, yield to God for insight and direction. Discern your teen's readiness before offering guidance.

Especially when the subject matter may be delicate in nature or awkward for an adolescent, mom and dad may not be a kid's go-to person. In our home, when our kids began to date, they were asked to have a mentor with whom they were willing to meet on a regular basis. A mentor gave them one more person who would ask hard questions and dispense wisdom as needed.

When we pursue an adolescent's heart by responding to their verbal, emotional, or behavioral cry to be heard, we validate the existence of this desire. Over time our interactions give us the opportunity to hold out essential truths about longings and the God who placed them within each of us.

RELAY Critical Truths

We crave what Adam and Eve experienced in the garden—unhindered and uninhibited communication with their Maker. They spoke. He listened. He spoke, and they responded. I'm sure transcripts of their conversations would span the spectrum between ordinary and extraordinary. Though we will never fully experience this kind of open and ongoing dialogue outside of heaven, adolescents need to know that God gave them a voice to express themselves. They need not be ashamed of this desire. Instead, we can use our everyday conversations to impart key truths about this longing that lives within us.

Even if you spent all day, every day responding to your teen's cries to be heard, you would only minimally satisfy their longings. You are not and never will be enough. In fact, parents who sacrifice everything to be at the beck and call of their teens interfere with their ability to experience God's presence. When kids find themselves feeling unheard or misunderstood, many will look toward heaven in search of Someone who will always hear and understand their cries. Nothing they may do or say will ever confuse the One who created them. In fact, He delights in hearing what they have to say. The first truth they need to hear is this: **God listens to the voices of His children.**

Aside from regular reminders of this truth, we can powerfully demonstrate our belief in it by regularly praying with our kids. When they are down, lonely, troubled, confused, indecisive, scared, or stressed, talk to God with them. When they are excited, hopeful, and happy about life, tell God how grateful you are. Take every opportunity to talk honestly with the Father about what's on your heart.

As you converse with Him as you would a friend, let them see how approachable He is. Even if kids don't have a personal relationship with God, few will resist a parent's desire to pray with them. Ushering our kids into God's presence allows them to see that the Great Listener cares about what we have to say in times of joy as well as sorrow.

Another way to help our kids trust that God hears them is to read and talk about the many verses in the Bible that substantiate this truth. Here are a few favorites that are certainly worth discussing and digesting over dinner or devotions:

Even before a word is on my tongue,
behold, O Lord, you know it altogether.
Psalm 139:4

I sought the Lord, and he answered me
and delivered me from all my fears.
Psalm 34:4

But I call to God,
and the Lord will save me.
Evening and morning and at noon,
I utter my complaint and moan,
and he hears my voice.
Psalm 55:16–17

When you direct teens to Christ through His Word, prayer, and conversations about Him, you reinforce the truth that He hears and understands. You also quiet the voice of the enemy, who perpetually tells them no one cares.

The second truth our kids need to hear is this: **Because He made you to be heard, you will always long for people to listen to your heart.** Our kids need to own this desire for relationships and understand that it's not bad or sinful or a sign of weakness. An adolescent's need for other people steadily increases over time due to God's design. God uses these friendships to help our kids learn how to become more intimately connected with other people. To be heard and understood by another offers great freedom to a heart designed to be known.

Family is the primary place where children learn about relationships. As they enter adolescence, however, kids need to learn how to transfer these skills to outside relationships. Helping this happen can be tough when life gets busy. When we don't provide time and space for friendships to begin and blossom, we should expect our adolescents to appear sad or even irritable. Friendships with peers offer them a place to extend and receive a very different listening ear than our own. Outside of school relationships are necessary workrooms for them to learn how to talk about their hearts. They also learn the cost of unhealthy and/or destructive relationships.

Unfortunately, these friendships will also disappoint them—repeatedly. Their very best friends, their amazing girlfriends or boyfriends, their mentors, youth pastors, or teachers will repeatedly fall short. They will be ignored, slighted, misunderstood, condemned, and even silenced. You are also one of those people. No one but God is able to fully satisfy this need for relationship.

Some teens will seek the God they know to comfort them. However, repeated disappointments can lead them to hear and believe the enemy's murmurs: *No one cares what you have to say. You're invisible. You are so awkward. Shhh. You have nothing to offer. Shut up. Push it down. Quit trying. Don't say a thing, especially if it's painful.* They suppress their true thoughts, withdraw opinions, and even take themselves out of the ring of relationships so they don't feel the pain when others don't meet their deep desire to be heard.

"You've got to get back in the ring and keep looking for healthy relationships," I often say to my kids or those I counsel. Many fool themselves into thinking if they give up the search, the longing will somehow subside. Others begin to use extreme methods and destructive strategies or find ways to numb the subsequent pain. This desire to be heard should never give them permission to wound themselves or others.

A safe, transparent relationship with outside individuals might include a youth pastor, a coach, a mentor, a youth leader, or a counselor. These connections offer our kids another place for them to open up and share their struggles. Safe adults not only offer a listening ear but also model healthy relationships.

Like every heart cry, the longing to be heard and understood can only be fulfilled as our kids lean into God and look for community. Although only God ultimately fulfills it, this commission to parents written by Paul Tripp in his book *Age of Opportunity* sums up our call so well:

> The call of the Word is clear. With hearts filled with Gospel hope, we will question and probe, listen and consider, plead and encourage, admonish and warn, and instruct and pray. We will awake every day with a sense of mission, knowing that God has given us a high calling. We are walls of protection that God has lovingly placed around our teenagers. We are the eyes that he has given that they might see. So we converse and converse and converse.[3]

I pray that your conversations with the adolescents in your life beautifully reflect God's heart for them as they daily manage this core desire to be heard and understood.

Chapter 5

"Notice Me." I long to be seen, selected, and set apart.

Before the creation of the universe God thought of me. He fixed his gaze on me and chose me for himself. ... He did not choose me because I was holy or good but so that I might become holy and good.
— John Piper[1]

*But you are a chosen race, a royal priesthood,
a holy nation, a people for His possession,
so that you may proclaim the praises
of the One who called you out of darkness
into His marvelous light. 1 Peter 2:9 HCSB.*

Heather, a high school senior, was a leader, an athlete, and a loyal friend. She was the go-to person whenever her friends needed someone to listen. Both males and females leaned on her for advice. It secretly bothered her that her many guy friends never showed interest in her. In fact, she had never been on a date. Near the end of high school, Heather's desire to have a boyfriend consumed her mind and heart.

One day a distant "friend" of a friend messaged her through social media. He had noticed her in a picture and told her she was pretty. Finding his random comment strange, yet flattering, Heather messaged him back. A few flirtatious comments eventually prompted audio and then video conversations. Knowing her friends and family would criticize this relationship, Heather didn't tell anyone. However, when her parents noticed their social daughter retreating to her room for long periods of time, they asked for an explanation. Heather told them about her new friendship and assured them he was fine. Even though they remained a bit concerned, they decided to trust her judgment.

When Heather described this young man as her boyfriend, her parents again expressed concern. This time, she became indignant. She tearfully insisted it was her turn to have someone special in her life, and no one could keep her from talking to him. Although she hated the tension this decision created, she refused to let go of the attention she received from her online boyfriend. Now that she had defended him, she felt compelled to meet him in person. Instead of going to school one morning, Heather bought a bus ticket and travelled all day to his home.

Once she arrived, everything unfolded just as she'd imagined. The kind comments continued; the sweet smile and witty remarks all resembled the guy she'd been getting to know online. By evening, however, everything changed. Just before his parents came home, he led her to his basement bedroom and aggressively insisted she "shut up" so they wouldn't know she was there. He snatched her cellphone and insisted she engage in sexual acts. Heather feared for her life.

The next morning, to keep her from running away, he tied her wrists to a desk and threatened to harm her if she left. Too afraid to move, she submitted to his every demand. Fortunately, within forty-eight hours, she was rescued by law enforcement. The young man was immediately arrested, and Heather, thankfully, survived the ordeal. The emotional and physical trauma she endured would take years to overcome.

In his book *The Soul of Shame*, Curt Thompson writes, "We all are born into the world looking for someone looking for us, and that we remain in this mode of searching for the rest of our lives."[2] While he is primarily referring to an infant's need to attach to a primary caregiver, adolescents repeat or mirror many of the developmental processes of early childhood. As they begin to separate from caregivers, adolescents look for other people who, in a sense, are looking for them as well. They long to be seen and selected in a special way. These social attachments often boost their sense of self. They also provide them with the courage needed to eventually detach and define themselves apart from parents.

This journey can take a teen down many paths. Heather was acutely aware of her longing to be deemed special. In sessions with me, she repeated-

ly stated her amazement that she would have gone
against so many beliefs and principles in order to satisfy this desire. But once she felt fulfilled in a way she
had never experienced before, she easily dismissed every conviction.

While relationships with the opposite sex are
probably the most significant way in which kids long
to be seen and selected, many other ways satisfy this
desire. Getting attention from a teacher, making the
cut from a coach, getting the lead as a part of a pro-
duction, or winning a coveted award can all gratify
this heart core desire.

Surprisingly, the outcome or the selection can be
rather ordinary. For example, many kids beam when
they share stories of being noticed by someone—anyone really—such as a band member who looks their
way during a concert or a popular student who mo-
mentarily acknowledges them in a hallway. In that
tiny gap in time, they feel singled out from others
around them.

In his book *Falling Upward*, Richard Rohr elabo-
rates on the power of the gaze.[3] He notes how intimate visual connections like these actually mirror the
Great Divine Gaze. Only Adam and Eve fully experienced the affectionate gaze of the Father as they interacted with Him in the most natural way possible.
The locked-on-never-ending gaze was tragically dis-
rupted, however, when the serpent turned their gaze
away from Him and toward something deceptive.

Erika Morrison writes, "Deceit slithered along and spoke in the garden and drew the eyes of those first children away from the Parent-gaze, the gaze that had guarded them entirely and reflected back their honest, love-consumed beings."[4] In that moment, mankind would forever search for the look from someone else that would remind them of their true selves and assure them of their special status.

When kids are offered the opportunity to be selected, in essence, they are searching for something distinct about them. They are looking for someone whose eyes, expression, or actions say, *I see you* and *I have chosen you.*

RECOGNIZE the Cry

My boys have been competitive with each other since the day the youngest could walk. "Who is faster, Mommy?" "Whose jump was splashier?" If they could possibly trump the other in some way, they did it. This desire surfaces in many sibling relationships. It also appears in many of the activities that occupy adolescents. Athletics, academics, visual and performing arts, as well as interests and hobbies—all offer the possibility of being able to stand out in some way.

In a culture where everything imaginable competes for attention, kids crave being seen as special. I have never heard a kid rejoice in feeling invisible or unacknowledged. As social creatures created for connection, the mere possibility of being rejected causes great angst. Their desperate attempts to avoid inattention will lead them along different paths in order to be seen and selected. Some of the most common strategies include the following.

Stepping out, stepping on, or standing out

In every adolescent peer group or subgroup, both spoken and unspoken rules exist. Kids take note, learn from others, and often step out beyond their comfort zones in order to stand out. Some kids will disregard the social norms and do whatever it takes to get noticed. They will step on others. They will embarrass, squelch, put down, or even cheat competitors in order to steal the attention. Sometimes, this tendency is even encouraged and modeled by the adults in their midst. Selfish and mean-spirited behaviors serve to substantiate this desire to stand out; however, they also serve as powerful reminders of what a person is capable of doing in order to ease the ache coming from the heart cry to be noticed.

Teens often use clothing styles to stand out. Black, shiny, lacy, skimpy, tattered, daring, or offensive clothing—you name it, and somebody is wearing it. Personal tastes may dictate their choices; however, for many, adolescents clothing, jewelry, make-up, and hairstyles reflect the attention they hope to receive. Just ask a female what she plans to wear on the first day of school. Many have thought long and hard about this decision. They want to be seen in just the right way.

Flirting through flaunting or displaying private areas of the body

As teens sexually mature, most long to be viewed as physically desirable—handsome or beautiful. In an increasingly sexualized world, many females (and males) believe that in order to be acknowledged by the opposite sex, they must flaunt their sexuality by posing or walking in highly sexualized ways or revealing more of their bodies. Many tell me that being discrete or modest only ensures that they will blend in and receive little to no attention. Movies, the media, and, in particular, television reality shows reinforce these beliefs. As a result, females wear provocative clothing to invite others to look with the secret hope of being chosen. Males wear pants around their hips, revealing their underwear.

The Internet perpetuates this philosophy by providing an avenue for adolescents to easily put themselves on display. Skyrocketing numbers of teens and young adults regularly use smartphone dating apps like Tinder, MyLOL, JCrush, and others to capitalize on this heart core desire to be selected. They openly allow others to view their pics and profile information so they can meet and possibly even "hook up."

Sending sexually provocative pictures or videos is yet another easily accessible means for gaining attention. According to the Pew Research Center, a majority of teens ages thirteen to seventeen have flirted with someone to let them know they were interested.[5] Of this group, ten percent said they sent flirty or sexy pictures or videos of themselves. Many studies suggest teens behave this way because they feel pressured—or believe it's necessary—to begin or maintain a relationship.

Tolerating abuse

According to a federally funded study, approximately 650 youths—almost twenty percent of both boys and girls in the study—reported themselves as victims of physical and sexual abuse in dating relationships. When the researchers defined psychological abuse, more than sixty percent of each gender said they had been both victim and perpetrator. Teens viewed antagonistic behaviors such as name calling, teasing, and accusations of flirting as acceptable—even necessary—in romantic relationships. Researchers noted "that girls perpetrate serious threats or physical violence more than boys at ages 12-14, but boys become the more common perpetrators of serious threats or physical violence by ages 15-18."[6]

These statistics support the fact that many teens are confused about what constitutes healthy dating relationships. Some believe that to attract or keep the gaze of another, they must tolerate destructive and abusive behavior. Being noticed requires them to be treated poorly.

Protecting the heart by minimizing the desire

Instead of grieving the loss or rejection, teens may minimize or even mock the desire to be noticed. *Who needs a relationship anyway? I don't really care if I win or not.* This tactic shields the heart from the possibility of disappointment. It may be used when a parent seems to repeatedly favor one sibling over another; a romantic interest won't give a teen the time of day; a teacher or coach constantly chooses other students for a special role; or an honor goes to another.

The proper response to any one of these situations is sorrow. Without permission from themselves or others to grieve, adolescents will often try to dampen the hurt by convincing themselves that being special is not necessary. Then they don't have to confront the deep pain of their hearts. The deepest wounds of adolescence frequently come from not being selected.

To want to receive that gaze—to be seen as special and wonderfully unique—is woven into our fibers by the God who sees us (Gen. 16:13). With a desire to experience this feeling in an earthly relationship, every teen I know wants to be chosen repeatedly by her mom and dad. In addition, she wonders who else really sees her as special. Even if she refuses to admit the presence of this desire, the pain of rejection will eventually remind her of its powerful presence.

RESPOND in a Helpful Manner

As parents or caring adults, we can look at our teens without really seeing them. Where we place our attention matters to our kids. It communicates what is most important to us. In order to get our attention, our kids may seek to make us proud or behave in extreme or inappropriate ways. We must be willing to take the time to notice them and then tell them what we see.

See them—acknowledge their presence.

A few years ago, Disney World hired cultural anthropologist, Kare Anderson, to analyze what grabbed the attention of young children at their theme parks and hotels in Orlando, Florida. In an article in the *Harvard Business Review*, Anderson highlights their findings: "Those kids clearly understood what held their parents' attention—and they wanted it too ... When parents were using their phones, they were not paying complete attention to their children." [7]

It's hard to believe that a parent's cellphone actually trumped everything Disney had to offer. By repeatedly focusing on something other than their kids, these parents were teaching their children what is worthy of our gaze. A better option is to put down the phone and with our eyes and facial expressions communicate, "I see you and I value you." When they see delight, awe, and pure joy in our faces, they know they have been noticed again. These connections have the power to reflect the gaze of the Father while also offering a visual model for what adoration looks like.

We were recently reminded of this power with our own daughter. She described her fondness for a young man she eventually married. I asked if she believed he felt the same about her. I will never forget her response: "Well, I see his face light up the same way your faces do whenever he looks at me; I've never seen a guy look at me the way he does." She recognized the meaning of that special, adoring gaze. She knew he viewed her as precious, unlike anyone else.

With busy schedules and a never-ending list of tasks, looking at our teenagers with delight can be extremely challenging. We have so much in front of us that noticing our precious kids is really hard. Not only that, our precious kids sometimes drive us crazy! Their less than desirable attitudes and actions can make it tough to want to grant them any of our attention. But God uses people to deliver His gaze. He can even use a tired and frustrated parent who is yielded to Him.

Select them.

"I pick you." Whether our kids have siblings or not, they want to feel set apart from others. Special time with each child may be easier when they are younger, but it remains just as important during the adolescent years. All of them still want to know that you are pleased that God chose them to be yours. Spontaneously or intentionally invite each child to accompany you on special trips or help you with special projects. Even if your teen doesn't openly express positive feelings about spending one on one time with you, pursue them anyway. While you are together, make a special effort to listen to your child.

A friend shared how she and/or her husband spend focused time with each of their six kids once per month on their birth date. For example, a child born on April 14 goes out with either mom or dad on the fourteenth of each month. These dates are simple, uncomplicated moments to look, listen, and love their kids well. Other families plan special ceremonies with each child when they hit milestone birthdays. These are intentional ways to gaze at our kids—to communicate how prized they are. I especially recommend special times for dads and daughters. Every girl dreams of someday being chosen by a man. A dad who adores his daughter sets a critical standard for future relationships.

Separate your pain from their pain.

Our own stories and feelings about rejection can easily become intertwined with those of our children. Their negative experiences trigger feelings and fears we experienced at some point. For example, we recall the year we tried out but didn't make it, or the boy or girl who picked our best friend over us, or the dance we attended alone. Before we know it, we're reliving the pain and making sure our kids never have to go through what we did. Unfortunately, this approach doesn't help teens learn to individuate their lives and losses from ours.

Separate your desires from theirs.

Over the years, I've counseled several kids who decided for various reasons they no longer wanted to play a particular sport, participate in an activity, or even stay in a relationship. On one occasion a parent asked me to use future sessions to entice his child to reverse her decision. My refusal to condone or abide by his request led him to terminate counseling sessions altogether.

To help you gain some objectivity, process your feelings and concerns with a trusted friend who can help you assess the situation more objectively.

Invite your kids to grieve when they are rejected.

When hearts are shattered, we want our kids to be happy again—to see the bright side of the loss. Quite often they will get there—but only after first being given permission to grieve. Even though God certainly desires that our kids ultimately place their hope in Him and His perfect plan, sorrow is the first stop along the way to peace.

When our kids face rejection or ache to be noticed by someone, the proper response is sadness. The passage through grief begins when a person first makes room in the heart to feel the loss. If we encourage her to dismiss or minimize the pain to protect her from experiencing loss, we're merely encouraging her to utilize defensive and/or self-protective measures to deal with the heart.

We don't want our kids to quench this heart cry to be noticed. Otherwise, they'll be robbed of experiencing the great Comforter who completely sympathizes with them. The kid who is actively searching to satisfy heart core desires is closer to landing in God's lap for consolation than the kid who convinces himself he doesn't need anything or anyone. By reflecting the compassion of the Father, we can validate the depth of rejection he feels, yet mirror His mercy. After all, more than anyone, God understands the pain of being cast aside. His own son was spat upon, repeatedly rejected, and then killed.

Your genuine compassion and quiet presence can be a balm of comfort that reflects Him and provides a visible anchor in the midst of their storms. When we can empathize, yet fully rest in God's providence, teens are more likely to do the same. If we become resentful or emotionally dramatic, then we communicate that this oversight is somehow outside of God's plan. We must teach our kids to manage the longings of their hearts by resting in Him. The psalmist said, *Be still, and know that I am God* (Ps. 46:10). We may never know why He allows certain events to occur. But we can trust that He is good all of the time, even when this cry of the heart remains unsatisfied.

When they get noticed, help them give God the glory.
We love to glory in ourselves—to bask in our own achievements. When God allows our kids to be acknowledged in some special way, we need to teach

them to offer Him the glory first. *Every good and perfect gift is from above,* writes James (Jas. 1:17 NIV). Any attention, praise, or acknowledgement helps our kids look to the One who allowed it to happen. Automatic responses such as "God is so kind to have given that to you" or "Praise God for blessing you with this favor" can remind a kid to first give God the glory. These statements can also take the pressure off the kid who feels overly burdened to continually achieve and places it in the hands of God.

Lead them to notice others.

From the homeless man to the kid who sits alone at lunch, our teens can be reminded to tune in to those around them who also want to be seen and selected. Part of helping our kids live in community means actively teaching them the importance of prizing others with their eyes, their words, and even their time. This means looking up from a digital device. It means giving proper attention to those who cross your path, even if no one does it for you. As they learn to offer to others what they deeply desire for themselves, they begin to practice trusting the Father to hear and satisfy the cries of their own hearts.

This action is particularly helpful when they can sacrificially applaud others who receive attention, recognition, or a coveted relationship. Helping our kids to humbly offer congratulatory words is critical to spiritual growth. Not only that, their words of praise testify to what it means to trust the Lord with your whole heart.

We want our kids to experience the temporal pleasures that often come with being picked. While I could say this about all eight desires, adults can unknowingly send a mixed message. We must always remember that the most important selection, the one that holds eternal value, comes from being seen and selected by God. Being prized as His child is the most important acknowledgement our kids can receive. We must mindfully maintain this perspective as we cheer them on or grieve with them over their losses.

RELAY Critical Truths

If God has woven this heart cry to be seen and selected into his existence, then each teen is hoping someone besides Mom or Dad will notice and choose him. A few will wonder if they will ever be picked in any form. Add to this their growing awareness of the vast world in which we reside, with over seven billion people vying for attention. We must make certain that our kids hear us say that *the Creator of the Universe— their Father in heaven—always sees them.*

The LORD looks down from heaven;
he sees all the children of man;
from where he sits enthroned he looks out

on all the inhabitants of the earth,
he who fashions the hearts of them all
and observes all their deeds.
Ps. 33:13–15

He observes their actions, perceives each thought, intimately knows their feelings, and understands every single longing. He fully sees, fully knows, and fully loves anyway. He prizes their uniqueness more than anyone because He created each of them. And, nothing—not even their sin—can disrupt the ability to be seen and loved by God.

When Hagar, an Egyptian slave, fled because of the abuse of Abram's wife Sarai, she encountered God in the desert. After receiving His comfort and encouragement, Hagar *called the name of the Lord who spoke to her, "You are a God of seeing," for she said, "Truly here I have seen him who looks after me"* (Gen. 16:13). Even though she ran away out of fear, God acknowledged her and told her that He had a unique plan for her son, Ishmael.

While many kids will take great comfort in being completely seen and known by God— even in our weakest moments—others will find this idea terrifying. If God sees and knows everything about us, then surely he will judge or condemn us instead of choosing and treasuring us. This tension didn't exist prior to sin entering the world. Guilt and shame began to color the freedom that comes from being fully seen.

For this reason, Adam and Eve covered themselves and hid in fear after they disobeyed God. This fear remains in each of us. But so does the longing to be seen, known, and prized.

We must also tell our teens that **His followers are holy and set apart.** His favor lies on those who have believed in the name of His Son Jesus and have surrendered their lives to His lordship. Paul writes, *Blessed be the God and Father of our Lord Jesus Christ, who has blessed us in Christ with every spiritual blessing in the heavenly places, even as he chose us in him before the foundation of the world, that we should be holy and blameless before him* (Eph. 1:3–4). God says, before you even knew me, I knew and chose you! This truth will always be enough for that large space in the hearts of our teens that aches to be seen and selected.

A relationship with the Lord eternally satisfies teens' desirous hearts. However, as long as they are here, the relentless nagging to be seen and set apart in earthly relationships or in areas that matter to them will continually surface. This longing is part of God's plan to draw them toward intimate relationships while simultaneously drawing them to Him. We must teach them to hold these desires in tension with the reality that God will satisfy their desires in His way and in His time.

When we see them repeatedly get passed over, we must combat deceptive or destructive statements with the truth of God's Word. Otherwise, the sorrow and frustration that accompanies painful experiences can easily send a kid into a tailspin. On earth our teens will never get picked as much as they desire. And, even if they did, worldly attention will never satisfy. Our God has

> set apart the godly for himself;
> the LORD hears when [they] call to him. Ps. 4:3

At the end of the day, this is and always will be more than enough.

Charles Spurgeon summarized the benefits that come from being chosen when he wrote so long ago:

> God has set apart His people from before the foundation of the world to be His chosen and peculiar inheritance. We are sanctified in Christ Jesus by the Holy Spirit when he subdues our corruptions, imparts to us grace, and leads us onward in the divine walk and life of faith.[8]

Celebrate His mercy, which enables us to be seen. Communicate this truth, for even in the church our kids often miss what it means to be chosen by God. As your teens openly talk and dream about being seen and selected, remind them of the reality of this blessing: God picked you.

Chapter 6

"Affirm Me." I wonder what I am worth.

It is difficult to make a man miserable while he feels worthy of himself and claims kindred to the great God who made him.
— Abraham Lincoln[1]

For you formed my inward parts;
you knitted me together in my mother's womb.
I praise you, for I am fearfully and wonderfully made.
Wonderful are your works;
my soul knows it very well.
My frame was hidden from you,
when I was being made in secret,
intricately woven in the depths of the earth.
Psalms 139:13–15

Jim was the kid many parents dream of rearing—academically and athletically gifted, handsome, and morally upright. Jim finished his first year of college in true Jim form: he made straight A's and found a great group of friends. By the end of his sophomore year, however, an unexpected breakup with his girlfriend and difficulties in several key classes became more than he could bear. This cheery young man was now sullen, tearful, and insecure.

When I first met Jim, he talked at length about his perceived academic and social failures. When I asked him to describe his problem, he responded, "I don't feel good about me when I'm not doing well." He added that he needed to find a way to boost his self-esteem.

Like many young people, Jim linked his value to achievements. But when difficulties arose, he battled waves of anxiety, which led him to strive harder. When this strategy failed, he began to question his worth. Surely, boosting his self-esteem would insulate him from feeling so badly about himself.

Unless Jim discovers the true foundation for his worth as a human being, his attempts to feel affirmed will be based on vacuous self-talk that will never target the real problem. My harsh prediction comes not just from personal and professional experience but also from sound research by individuals who were curious about the real impact of the self-esteem movement. This movement began in the early '70s following the release of a book entitled *The Psychology of Self-Esteem* by Nathaniel Branden.

Heavily influenced by Ayn Rand, Branden observed that confident people tend to believe they are worthy of happiness and more effectively "cope with the basic challenges of life."[2] As a result, he theorized that if a kid's self-esteem were boosted throughout development, he would be happier and more successful as well. Almost overnight, Branden's theories turned into a call to action, which massively popularized the notion of self-esteem. Eventually, every policy, principle, or practice regarding the welfare of children was impacted by this new buzzword. If confidence could be conferred upon children by boosting their self-esteem, then the child, family, community, and nation would prosper.

After decades of the self-esteem movement, we now know that higher self-esteem doesn't appear to improve academic or job performance, leadership skills, or healthy habits; nor does it prevent children from smoking, drinking, using drugs, or engaging in early sex.[3] Furthermore, some of the research actually reveals that kids reared during the last forty years are significantly more self-centered, disrespectful, anxious, and depressed than ever.[4]

As it turns out, kids who are solely given positive feedback lose the ability to know how their efforts really compare to others. Over time, this seems to contribute to less confidence, less resilience, and an overall diffused sense of self that makes dealing with losses, rejections, and disappointments more difficult. These kids disguise their insecurity with an entrenched arrogance, projecting an overly inflated and/or demanding self to others. When enormous challenges arise—and their best efforts aren't enough to carry them through—kids like Jim end up experiencing intense bouts of anxiety linked to their inability to measure up.

While many articles, research reports, and books have been written about the flaws of this movement and the ideologies associated with it, from a biblical worldview, we shouldn't be surprised by the problems it created. A formulaic and rather meaningless system of praise and affirmation can't somehow confer a deep sense of value to an individual.

Every human being wants to know the answer to the question, *am I valuable?* We also want to know *why am I valuable?* Without offering a viable answer, people will base their worth on some standard other than the value bestowed by God. Self-esteem without the inclusion of God becomes a rather phony, hollow, or vacillating state instead of a steadfast confidence based on biblical truths.

RECOGNIZE the Cry

When discussing longings with kids I counsel, the search for their value is typically one of the top two that consumes them and drives many of their choices. Knowing how they pursue or naturally receive affirmations from others is critical information for any parent or caring adult. This awareness can open up opportunities to have ongoing conversations that allow you to affirm them while still reflecting and conveying God's truths about their intrinsic worth.

The most common inclinations associated with this cry are listed below. Even if teens have a personal relationship with God and believe their value is ultimately founded in Him, these are the areas that may tempt them the most.

Obsessed with appearance

Overall size or appearance consumes many teens. They rely on these to make them feel worthy. If the praise doesn't come—or they believe something about them doesn't look right— feelings of insecurity abound. Eating and exercise disorders continue to be one of the many ways adolescents strive to receive affirmation. Contrary to popular belief, this tendency is not limited to females. One longitudinal study demonstrated that "a considerable number of adolescents experience body dissatisfaction, and that the variables that increase risk are analogous regardless of gender." [5]

The media's portrayal of the ideal man and woman can certainly distort a teen's self-image. Regular exposure to these images definitely shapes one's standard for beauty. While nothing is wrong with looking and feeling healthy and beautiful, be alert to the teen whose mood and actions seem heavily impacted by what they see in the mirror or read on the scale. These may be a cue that they're trying to manage the longing for value by looking the right way.

Fixated on accomplishments

Do you know the kid who seems to win every prize, earn every title, and gain the attention of teachers, coaches, judges, and peers? These kids are often described as driven, diligent, determined, and dependable. They work hard and strive for excellence. Getting that grade, making the team, or receiving recognition makes them feel so good that they can't imagine not attaining their goals. Parents, teachers, and coaches tend to love these kids.

However, for many the more they are praised, the more they fear failure. The idea of disappointing themselves or anyone else can cause them to be a slave to perfectionism. These kids often struggle with a good measure of anxiety, restlessness, and even depression. Sadly, many work hard to disguise these emotions by projecting a calm and composed exterior to those around them. Inside, some overachievers base their worth on what they do.

Consumed by possessions

Similar to the *right* look, some kids are driven to possess the *right* brand of clothing or other luxury item in order to feel affirmed or worthy. Having the latest digital gadget—the right cell phone, laptop, or iPad—brings them the status or the compliments they crave. Around the globe, the adolescent consumer drives product development, marketing, and ad campaigns. Catering to the wishes and wants of this group is a multi-billion dollar enterprise. American teens have money in their pockets, and, if they don't, they know how to manipulate the wallets of their parents.

Consumerism can easily lure our kids into thinking they need some *thing* to feel good about themselves. But since the pleasure is fleeting, the need for possessions becomes a vicious cycle propelled by passing highs and perpetual lows. Those kids you know who want the newest and best may have come to believe that their worth is based on what they hold in their hands instead of on the One whose fingerprints are all over them.

Mastered by morality

This description may sound confusing at first. Of course we want our kids to live morally upright lives, especially as believers. But I've met plenty of adolescents who have inadvertently attached their value to their moral way of living. In a wholehearted effort to please God and/or their parents, they believe that as long as they do the *right* thing, live the *right* way, or say the *right* response, all with a pleased look on their faces, they are worthy. Often, their peers view them as haughty, self-righteous, or superior.

To the parent of a defiant or rebellious kid, this super saint may hardly sound like a problem. But if you have a teen obsessed with living a morally blameless life, you understand this dilemma. When they fail to live up to a prescribed standard, which they will in some way at some point, these kids feel they have lost their value. They may greatly struggle to understand the true meaning of grace and forgiveness, especially with regard to themselves.

Because adolescents are growing up in a world that doesn't recognize their value or worth from a biblical perspective, most will likely seek the affirmation of others by relying on one or more of these methods. So many kids are living life in overdrive that getting off the treadmill means they may face a dearth of approval or affirmation. So, they convince themselves to appear, perform, achieve, obtain, or avoid so they can hear the praise they crave.

Who can blame them? If most of us are honest, we may actually be perpetuating the problem. Perhaps we inadvertently reinforce their beliefs and encourage them to get back on that treadmill. Or, maybe we have tried to affirm them with truth, but we send mixed messages. Our own lifestyle doesn't communicate or model what we're saying. For this reason, parents and caring adults must strive to be more intentional about responding to their cries in a consistent way that communicates the value God has placed on them.

RESPOND in a Helpful Way

If we don't regularly validate our teens' existence, worth, thoughts, feelings, viewpoints, or whatever is unique about them, they will look in other directions for what they long for, even if these avenues are unpredictable and unattainable. While all core desires can certainly lead to idolatry (as we will discuss in more detail in Chapter 13), the Creator placed within our children the wish to be affirmed. A dearth of affirmation in any kid's life can negatively influence him to lean on one of four aforementioned arenas to feel valued or worthy.

Balance compliments with the day-to-day commands, corrections, and criticisms given.
Social media platforms offer instant validation and approval. When teens post a cute picture or a witty remark, others weigh in with their *likes* or comments. I often hear my kids marvel over the number of *likes* a certain post or picture receives. While these numbers may seem meaningless or unimportant to us, for adolescents they offer multiple avenues of affirmation.

In this arena, however, rarely do our kids hear their peers affirm character or effort. If we are honest, many don't hear this in our homes either. Instead, they hear us commanding, correcting, or even criticizing: "Pick up your shoes." "Stop treating your sister that way." "You need to work on your attitude." We can get so caught up in the areas that need correction that we overlook their efforts, progress, or growth in character. We forget that most of our kids experience a good bit of criticism from their peers, coaches, or teachers. They're looking for people who will say something kind and affirming about them. During family sessions, many kids share that they wish they could hear compliments, as well as correction, from their moms or dads.

Affirmation can be tough to do with a kid who repeatedly makes poor choices. Daily these kids hear what they're not doing right or how they need to change. You can always find a way to affirm them. Write notes or use words to encourage them. Remind them, especially when they fail, that they're still loved and valued by you.

Affirm inner beauty and character over outward appearance.

Assess how you act and what unspoken messages you send. When our kids enter the adolescent years, their maturing brain allows them to detect mixed messages or hypocritical expectations far more easily. Do they see you endlessly striving for perfection as a way of feeling good about yourself? For example, I regularly hear kids tell me how much their parents openly complain or obsess about their weight or appearance with their friends. They talk about diets, pills, or eating regimens under the guise of wanting to be healthy; yet, they seem to be communicating their own insecurity, as well.

Take time to examine the ways you may be searching for significance apart from God. Instead of trying to project something that isn't authentic, use your own struggle as an opportunity to talk about your desire to rest in God's truths instead of relying on something that will never fully gratify this desire. The way we live and our willingness to be open about our own difficulties in this area may be the best way to equip them for this ongoing battle.

In a world where eating disorders are prevalent, many parents ask me if they should avoid complimenting or even commenting on their adolescent's appearance. I respond that if your son or daughter looks handsome or beautiful, then tell them. Nothing is wrong with affirming our kids' outward appearance. In fact, I'm sure their heavenly Father is pleased with how lovely they are. More so, God values their inner beauty—their hearts, their character, their values. We must affirm the outward fruit or actions that arise out of their inward beauty, so that our kids are less inclined to seek praise for the way they appear on the outside.

With this in mind, when you see them demonstrating a fruit of the spirit (love, joy, peace, patience, kindness, goodness, faithfulness, self-control), be intentional about commenting on their actions. This demonstration of inner beauty is invaluable compared to someone whose flawless face and body veil a superficial, selfish, or entitled individual.

Use disappointments to discuss and defeat shame.

While I want my kids to strive for excellence, I pray that their worth isn't attached to the outcome. Teens can easily misconstrue our reminders to work hard as a statement that they must not fail. For this reason, our response to the inevitable disappointments they will experience is critical. When our kids miss the mark in some way, they will look to a parent, teacher, coach, instructor, team, or crowd to either substantiate or refute the *not good enough* or thoughts of failure that instantly pop into their minds.

For some kids, these and other shame-filled statements stir up fear and anxiety. In turn, these feelings will cause some to strive harder in order to hush the voices. For others, they lead to feeling crushed and defeated to the extent that they throw in the towel and quit. Shame, which is essentially the belief that you are flawed and worthless, has never been an effective motivator. Instead, it becomes a slave master, driving our kids toward perfectionism instead of renewed effort.

Talking about shame as it relates to performance and worth is the first step in disarming its power. When an adolescent knows that he is loved and inherently valued—even when he makes a mistake or experiences defeat—this unshakable sense of worth can provide him with the confidence to pick up again from where he left off. Think about the difference between the words *I can* and *I must*. The word *must* is propelled by fear and anxiety. The word *can* gives kids the freedom and choice to keep going. If they know their ultimate value before their parents or God is unshakeable, they're more likely to take healthy risks and face life's challenges with a measure of confidence.

Create mantras or short statements to resist lies.
Remember the phrase "I think I can, I think I can, I can" uttered by the Little Engine in the famous children's

story by Watty Piper? When the train was doubtful of its ability to get over the mountain, repeating four words boosted her confidence and helped her push through the task. While this example may seem juvenile and simplistic, the idea of meditating on truths to defeat lies is biblical.

Once I can help a teen identify the automatic thoughts that often pop into her mind, we spend time creating a short statement that she believes and is willing to repeat to herself whenever the voice of shame, defeat, or despair clouds her thinking. Common phrases include:

*God's plan will prevail.

*His way is perfect and right.

*He loves me as I am.

*When I'm weak, He's strong.

*This loss/defeat/moment doesn't define me.

*I am desirable.

*I am worthy because of Christ.

These truths have power against the lies that swim around inside our kids. Even if I affirm them all day long, they must learn how to affirm themselves by being rooted in God's truths. Then, when defeats arise, the enemy doesn't capitalize on their doubts.

Simplify instead of multiply.

Growing up in one of the wealthiest nations in the world makes it difficult to avoid consumerism. We can easily convince ourselves that we must have a certain gadget, brand, or possession of some sort. As you make decisions about purchasing items for yourself, your home, or your kids, consider how it may fuel instead of fight materialism. When kids see a parent or an adult who is perfectly content regardless of what he possesses, they learn that their satisfaction or contentment doesn't need to be attached to things. Learn to be firm and say *no* to the things you or your family don't really need.

This may sound obvious but asking a kid why she is obsessing over having something can lead her to talk about what may be fueling her wants. You can ask this question in many ways. I may ask, "What will life be like if you don't get what you want?" Quite often, I will hear kids say, "Terrible!" or "No, that won't happen because I won't let it!" Their answers may indicate a heart that is leaning on something fleeting, indefinite, and completely unable to fully satisfy their core desire to be affirmed.

When it comes to performance, prestige, possessions, or appearance, our kids must experience periods when they don't get what they desire. If we constantly fan the flames of striving—or rescue them from feeling deprived—we may hinder their search for the only One who can fully satisfy their longing to be seen as valuable and worthy.

RELAY Critical Truths

Like all core desires, the way our kids pursue affirmation tells us a lot about their understanding of God's truth. Spend time talking about what you see. The more we engage in dialogues—and even debates—about this longing within everyone, the more we actually affirm their desire to be valued. In the midst of these ongoing discussions, we can make it a point to communicate the most relevant truths about who they are before God and in Christ, as well as how they can find value in the context of community.

One of the best examples God has used to communicate a few key truths related to my worth comes from an antique painting I own. Oddly enough, I bought it solely for the antique frame that surrounded it. The painting is a gloomy picture of a ship in the midst of a storm. Sadly, the canvas has a large slice through it, which only adds to the depressing tone. Because I never chose to use the frame, the old painting remained attached to the frame, stored in a stack of pictures in our attic.

While we were cleaning out storage areas one year, my kids (who at the time were addicted to "The Antiques Roadshow" television program) encouraged me to have an appraiser look at it. Thinking the whole idea was a bit silly, I resisted. But when we discovered that an appraiser would be doing free assessments at a nearby mall, we decided to take it to him. After waiting in a very long line, I rather sheepishly took my painting out of a pillowcase and laid it on the table. Immediately, the man gasped. Feeling like we were actually on an episode of "The Antiques Roadshow," our hearts raced as we imagined what the value could be.

First, he told us it was a rare painting by an Irish painter, and he hadn't seen one like ours for some time. He took it out of the frame and educated us on the time period, the artist's technique, and even the subject of the painting. When he was done, he told us that even though it was damaged, he thought it could be worth a few thousand dollars. We couldn't believe it! Because of who created this dreadful painting, it actually had value.

My damaged painting offers a perfect metaphor to help you remember the critical truths we want to relay to our kids about their worth.

First, because they were formed by God and made in His image, teens are valuable. Each one needs to hear that he is *fearfully and wonderfully made* (Ps. 139:14), that he was formed *a little lower than the heavenly beings,* and crowned with *glory and honor* (Ps. 8:5). The name of the artist bestowed value upon my painting just as the Creator, who fashioned our children in the womb, gave each intrinsic value.

Like my antique painting, they are broken, imperfect, and damaged because of their sin nature. Although this doesn't take away their inherent value, it changes their status. In a world that wants our kids to think they're awesome and amazing, they need to know that their sin actually disrupts their ability to have a relationship with their Maker.

Just as I needed an expert craftsman to repair my artwork, our kids need someone who can mend their broken relationship with God. The perfect restorer came in the form of God's Son. He alone can rescue and redeem them. If your kids have acknowledged their brokenness and chosen to surrender their lives to Christ, they are seen as new creations and viewed by their Creator as righteous because of Christ's blood, which was shed for them.

Only in Christ are they deemed worthy before their Maker. Because of His death on the cross, their status or position can change from unworthy and undeserving to righteous and beloved. Make sure your kids know that being made in God's image makes them valuable, but only Christ's blood makes them worthy of standing before Him in heaven.

Second, most people can be placed into one of two groups: those who respect and build you up and those who deflate and devalue you. Because they crave affirmation, teens need a core group of friends throughout their lives who remind them of their true value and worth. Affirming words can help them stand firm. Ideally, this group is multigenerational and made up of family members, friends, and mentors. These people resemble those bumper pads that keep the bowling ball out of the gutter. Their words of encouragement prevent kids from giving up on themselves or on what God is calling them to do or be, especially when they are surrounded by negative people or treading difficult waters.

Help them come up with a list of about five people who regularly support and affirm them. Encourage them to meet with their supporters regularly. Ask the adults on the list if they will reach out to your kid when life gets tough. Also, consider being one of these people for the adolescents you know. When your teen sees willingness on your part to buoy up other kids, she may be even more open to having adults she knows to do the same.

Regularly hearing the truth about their value and worth can help any kid better detect and resist the plethora of lies around them. Instead of making choices to prove who they are or to strive endlessly to win the favor of others by what they have or hold, they can rest in the truth of being loved and deemed valuable by their Creator. I have these words by Robert McGee on a small index card in my office to remind my clients (and me) of the depth of God's love and favor for His children.

Because of *justification,* you are completely forgiven and fully pleasing to God. You no longer have to fear failure.

Because of *reconciliation,* you are totally accepted by God. You no longer have to fear rejection.

Because of *propitiation,* you are deeply loved by God. You no longer have to fear punishment, nor do you have to punish others.

Because of *regeneration,* you have been made brand-new, complete in Christ. You no longer need to experience the pain of shame.[6]

Let us live our lives believing, reflecting, and declaring these truths so that our kids will be secure, confident, and full of joy, knowing their worth can't be taken from them.

Chapter 7

"Befriend Me." I crave relationships.

Social Media—from Facebook to Twitter—have made us more densely networked than ever. Yet for all this connectivity, new research suggest that we have never been lonelier (or more narcissistic)—and that this loneliness is making us mentally and physically ill.
— Stephen Marche, "Is Facebook Making Us Lonely?"[1]

So then you are no longer strangers and aliens, but you are fellow citizens with the saints and members of the household of God, built on the foundation of the apostles and prophets, Christ Jesus himself being the cornerstone.
Ephesians 2:19–20

By the age of twelve, Gretchen had been repeatedly rejected and bullied by kids at her private Christian school for no apparent reason. To make matters worse, she felt misunderstood by several teachers, as well as the principal. After repeated attempts to advocate for their daughter, her parents decided to homeschool her. Being at home gave her the safety and respite she needed after enduring so much pain from her peers.

Although her online schooling provided her with virtual teachers and students, she never physically interacted with them. Other connections only existed online, as well. Every time her mother suggested she enroll in community activities, Gretchen's fear that the past would repeat itself kept her from committing.

When I met Gretchen, she admitted feeling disconnected but fiercely defended her desire to stay isolated: "You don't understand how bad it was. People always hurt me." At other times, Gretchen would sob, often uncontrollably, over her feelings of loneliness. She deeply longed to have what she believed everyone else had—friendships. Despite this, memories of her painful past kept her cornered.

Over time, Gretchen recognized that she must begin to move forward. Since nothing seemed to curb the core desire she now acknowledged, Gretchen finally decided to enroll in a class at the local college. She knew the connections she craved could only come by taking risks and choosing to be vulnerable. With two steps forward and one step back, she slowly learned how to stay in pursuit of relationships.

Gretchen's story reminds us of the importance of both family and peer connections. During a painful season of her life, her family provided her with a safety net—some space to heal while she continued school. Since families are meant to be the primary organization for belonging, home satisfied Gretchen's hunger for connection for a time.

As she approached adolescence, however, something within her ached to be part of a community outside her home as well. Her parents' love and affection had not changed. But her developmental needs fueled her desire to expand her friendships and connections with others. Gretchen's insightful awareness of this longing actually made her angry at times. She knew it would be much easier to remain connected solely to family. Internal changes, however, would not allow her to ignore this core desire.

One might assume that in a world of approximately twenty-five billion devices connected to the Internet, our desire for friendships would be abundantly satisfied.[2] Research, however, reveals that as the number of connecting gadgets rise, so do the numbers of people who report feeling lonely and depressed.[3] Despite our ability to talk, message, and video chat, the digital age may, in fact, play a central role in the growing disconnection and isolation occurring around the globe.

Proof appears everywhere you go. Look around at a waiting room, restaurant, spectator sport, or event. You see individuals, couples, or even families sitting side by side tuned into their gadgets instead of each other or the main event. Passively scrolling through their devices, they spend their idle time connecting with others by liking or commenting on images. Or, while sitting or standing beside actual people, they construct texts. Our dependence on these gadgets actually shields our ability to see what's right in front of us, thereby exacerbating the loneliness many people feel.

Made in the image of God, we're designed to have intimate relationships that go much deeper than anything a screen can offer. In Genesis 2:18 when God said, *It is not good that the man should be alone,* he meant for companionship to develop through face-to-face connections with others.

For some teens, these relationships will develop naturally and easily. Other kids' frustration with their inability to forge friendships may lead them to do anything for the sake of being included or befriended by another person or group. And many will give up or settle for the illusion of friendship brought to them in less than a second on a shiny screen.

RECOGNIZE the Cry

During the elementary school years, kids' friendships slowly begin to blossom. Regular interactions at school, neighborhood play, birthday parties, athletic teams, and other extracurricular activities help our kids learn how to create and keep a connection with another person. But even if these encounters are limited, as long as a child comes home to relatively healthy interactions between parents and siblings, most fare quite well.

Their contentment with few friendships begins to change as adolescent development progresses. The developmental shifts unfolding within them begin to necessitate the presence of steady and ongoing relationships with peers. The desire to be part of a group, a squad, a team, or a club should naturally increase as the changing brain and body begin to impact what they desire. For some, these changes almost provoke a sense of urgency or a state of emergency. They must be with a friend or a group of friends or life is terrible! At this point, the kid who never seemed to care about being with his peers will eventually become sorrowful, bitter, angry, or worried about having no friends.

During this transitional period, the drama surrounding friendships and/or exclusions can be unbearable for kids (and parents). Regardless, teens will slowly choose to trust others and spend more and more time with them. Whether the transition toward peer relationships is messy or smooth, the four most common behaviors associated with the cry to be befriended are listed below.

Attending social events and group experiences
The healthiest way for most kids to satisfy their longing for friendship is by increasingly spending more time with others their age. These encounters will help them further develop or tweak the relational skills they already have. Learning how to create connections, manage conflict, read facial expressions, and

tune into social cues can only happen as kids physically interact with others.

A teen's growing obsession to be with her peers is not a statement about how she feels about her mom, dad, or home. Instead, it indicates developmental growth and a genuine need to expand her community beyond her family. This inclination must be viewed as a positive. While parents may find driving kids around or hosting them in their homes exhausting, the need to cultivate friendships comes from a God-given desire.

Connecting through digital media

According to a recent survey by the Pew Research Center, seventy-three percent of teens now have a smartphone.[4] As a result, most kids rely on texting as one of their primary methods of communication. If they aren't texting, many are connecting with others through video game interchanges or through dozens of social media platforms like Facebook, Twitter, Instagram, Snapchat, Tumblr, YikYak, Medium, WhatsApp, GroupMe, Pinterest, or even dating apps like Tinder, MeetMe, Skout, or MyLOL. These apps are so prevalent among teens that one survey indicates that over half of the adolescent population has met at least one of their friends online.[5]

According to another study, the average American teenager (13-18 year olds) spends nine hours per day on entertainment media use excluding time spent at school and on homework. Tweens (8-12 year olds) use an average of six hours of entertainment media. "In sum, media are an enormous presence in young people's lives, a huge claim on their time and attention, and an element of their lives that is well worth our continued attention."[6]

We must remember that because of the massive brain development occurring during the adolescent years, these social habits actually shape the brain. John Cacioppo, author of the book *Loneliness* and director of the Center for Cognitive and Social Neuroscience at the University of Chicago, has conducted research to study the impact that decreased human interaction will have on gene expression. The Center's findings indicate that "loneliness affects not only the brain, then, but the basic process of DNA transcription. When you are lonely, your whole body is lonely.[7] His findings concur with other research that changes to the brain can be lasting and detrimental when an individual is not engaged in ongoing relationships.

Suddenly altering moral choices, interests, activities, or styles

The pressure to conform to the group in order to be included, accepted, or befriended has been around since sin entered the world. As the heart core desire for friendships steadily increases, an adolescent's temptation to engage in certain behaviors, or mimic attitudes, in order to be included will exponentially rise. An extreme shift in behaviors, a subtle change in their clothing styles, or a complete abandonment from previously held principles or beliefs—these can often be driven by this core desire to belong.

I have counseled many kids who told me the unhealthy, illegal, or risky activities they engaged in used to be on their *I would never* list. Then, wanting, needing, or aching to belong allowed the pendulum to swing in the other direction. The thought of isolation or disconnection motivated them to partake, be it consciously or unconsciously. Their assessment of the risk involved began to change, quieting any conviction and moving them toward conformity.

Conformity is one of the many ways that all humans seek inclusion or connection. And though some choices can certainly lead to negative outcomes, not all do. I can think of several kids who were pushed to a higher standard because of their peers. Others managed their negative impulsive tendencies better in order to avoid being shunned by a group. No doubt power exists with any group. For this reason, parents and caring adults should know as much as possible about the squads, flocks, crowds, or packs that exist within their teens' worlds and the expectations or reputations of each.

Excessively viewing reality shows, dramas, or series (Netflix, YouTube, Amazon, Hulu)

"Seven hours," she proudly exclaimed as she sat down in my office. When I questioned what she meant, she quickly explained that she had just spent seven hours catching up on her new favorite show. During times of stress, boredom, loneliness, or even despair, many kids cope by binge watching TV shows in this way. Limitless amounts of media available through so many formats can clearly have a negative impact on how this core desire to belong is satisfied—particularly for kids who have struggled to create or keep friendships.

Watching a screen can become an easy escape that quickly transports them into someone else's storyline. One of the reasons reality television shows have become so popular is by inviting the audience to vicariously experience the dramas of others. The experience can trick the mind into thinking that it has been with people for long periods of time. But nothing can fool the heart. Analyzing the lives of others from a comfortable distance by skimming through posts or viewing characters in a television series is a low risk and passive way to experience the vulnerability of others without having to take risks or expose oneself.

Relationships require courage, risk taking, exposure, and practice. When an adolescent spends an inordinate amount of time watching show after show instead of actually relating, they may actually be trying to gain the benefits of belonging without taking any risks. Watching people on a screen requires no sacrifice and, therefore, offers few, if any, benefits.

Though our kids may downplay the effect that hour after hour has on their capacity or willingness to relate, being repeatedly exposed to immature standards of conduct can and will shape the way they view themselves, others, and relationships in general. Moreover, while it may be argued that something can be gained from these shows or digital media, this activity offers little but a break from real connection.

RESPOND in a Helpful Manner

The following three essential needs of teens must be met in order for them to establish close relationships. First, kids need parents who model friendship with each other and with others in the community. Second, they need families who intentionally spend focused time together so they can acquire the basic tools for human connection. Third, they need friends outside of their homes who include them, who want to know them, and who want to be known by them. We play a vital role in fostering these kinds of relationships by the way we model and encourage healthy friendships with others.

Place reasonable limits on media use.

Our society has been duped into thinking that digital conversations can actually resemble or even replace time spent with another person. Since interpersonal skills develop by spending time with others, kids who heavily depend on texts, messages, online chats, or media posts to communicate may never receive what the heart really needs. While these applications make it easy to feel connected, they don't offer the emotional and social satisfaction that come through time spent in live interaction. Kids who engage with others in this way often demonstrate marked deficits in their interpersonal skills. They'll have more difficulty forging genuine connections.

Intimacy, authenticity, reconciliation, and healing cannot be learned by interacting with screens. Our teens must see, feel, and experience these exchanges before their very eyes. When they actually sit in the messiness, the silence, tension, or discomfort—instead of dodging it through the use of digital devices—they'll slowly become accustomed to the critical elements of genuine human connections. They'll assimilate skills and a comfort level central to maintaining relationships.

Interestingly, Sherry Turkle, M.I.T. professor and author of several books on the intersection of culture and technology, substantiates this possibility by stating that our increased dependence on technology actually appears to be increasing our fear—instead of ease—with deep relationships. In her popular TED Talk video, she remarks:

> We're lonely, but we're afraid of intimacy. And so from social networks to sociable robots, we're designing technologies that will give us the illusion of companionship without the demands of friendship. We turn to technology to help us feel connected in ways we can comfort-

ably control. But we're not so comfortable. We are not so much in control.[8]

As humans, our kids will always long for *ties that bind*. But their dangerous dependence on creating these through technology can actually deprive them of the very thing they crave.

I am often asked, how much is too much screen time when it comes to adolescents and the brain? Neuroscience research most certainly suggests that they need time away. The heart of the issue is, in a given day how much awake time do your kids spend completely unplugged? What our kids desperately need is time spent with one another—face time—the original way. Only as your kids learn to spend quality time with each other will they experience the connection that comes from playfulness, laughter, and heartfelt discussions, as well as peaceful silence. Skills and habits and conversational tools gained through real life relationships will give them the raw materials for cultivating the long-lasting connections they were made for.

Another question is, how much does your family talk and relate to one another without the involvement of a screen or digital device? Resist the temptation to give in to the norm, and fight for uninterrupted and undistracted time with your kids, with your spouse, and with your family as a unit. The resistance you may face pales in comparison to the fruit this time can yield. Teens may not advocate for this time together, but I know many who have told me they're grateful for their parent's commitment to relationships. Determine to do it, set the limits, and seize the opportunities.

Get to know your kid's village.

Peer pressures vary from setting to setting and group to group. No parents or caring adults can be fully informed about the subtle or overt pressures that surround a kid. However, intentional conversations can help. Connect with parents whose kids are at school with yours. These encounters can happen naturally at athletic or extracurricular events, while working together at school functions, or by spending time with other families whose kids attend the same school. Don't allow the information you gain to instigate fear or to provoke inquisition sessions with your kid. Instead, allow it to arouse compassion and impress a need for ongoing connection and conversation with your own child.

One of the best ways I have learned about my kid's village comes through interacting with their peers. During carpools, time spent at our home, and in leisure activities, other teens are often more open to talk to me about the stresses in their lives. Hearing them chat about certain people or situations gives me a broader sense of specific pressures they face in order to belong. If I can stay quiet and ask a few pointed questions without making judgments, they typically open up even more.

Recently, a few of my son's friends came over. While cleaning up the kitchen, two girls I barely knew began to talk about "disgusting guys" at school. After quietly wiping counters and loading dishes, I interjected a statement of sympathy: "That must be so hard to hear all the time." Instead of being offended, they continued with more examples. That evening I gained a new perspective on some of the battles my son had alluded to but never fully described. I also understood why he had been distancing himself from certain kids whom I had previously perceived as stand up kids at the school. My compassion increased and so did my confidence in his selection of peers.

The bottom line is that we don't really know much about their peer groups and the pressure to conform unless we make an effort. Since being connected is so critical and because they need the support and guidance of caring adults to help them with these relationships, we ought to know a bit about the people in their villages.

Provide a place for your kids' friends to hang out.
To help you know your kids' village and to guide them in their connections, encourage them to invite their friends to your house. You will need to be willing to offer food and a comfortable space. You must also be willing to overlook some messes. If you help their friends feel welcomed and safe, then your children may be the ones who lead the way in making your home their favorite hangout. This doesn't mean

that rules, expectations, or boundaries get thrown out of the window. Instead, your reasonable expectations remind them that you are still supervising, even if you remain on the periphery.

These occasions give you a front seat and an ear to the drama, as well as the delights, of their friendships. Your observations can help you both understand and guide your own kid with regard to their longing for friendship. Find time to make positive observations about their group of friends. Our kids need our insights and are most receptive when these are shared with grace and sensitivity.

Foster family connections through outings and traditions. Break away from the rhythm of life by leaving town for the day, a weekend, or a week. Outings offer families a respite from the chaos and disconnection of daily life. Time spent outdoors, discovering a new place, attending an entertainment event, or building a family tradition can foster a deep sense of belonging among your brood. Involve your kids in the planning process so they feel included in the activity. If they aren't excited about the destination, invite them to pick special trips or adventures for another time.

Although bringing friends of kids along may keep the peace, consider the greater need. If you want your kids to experience healthy connections within your home, try to balance the times you invite extras with trips made up of just your family. Both can offer benefits. Consider the goal for the getaway and decide how guests would benefit or intrude upon the desired outcome.

If you have more than one child, encourage the siblings to get together without their parents. My husband and I found this approach strengthened the connection between our children. Because they are the only ones who understand what it is like to be a Perry kid, looking for ways to unite them increased their sense of belonging in our home.

Encourage connections with extended family.

Growing up as the daughter of first-generation immigrants, I spent very little time with extended family. The few visits we had, however, impacted me greatly. I felt more connected to my family overseas. Their unabashed affection for me was just what I needed during my *who am I and where do I belong* years. Although I rarely saw them, I knew that these roots were deep. When periods of loneliness or disconnection hit me hard, my connection to my greater family carried me through.

Extended American families rarely live in the same communities anymore. Because some kids feel a lack of belonging in their nuclear families, a connection with a cousin, an aunt, uncle, or grandparent can go a long way. These relationships begin through family vacations, holidays, or frequent visits. Notice those relatives whom your kids enjoy or with whom they identify. Ask the relative to reach out to your child in some way. Because of the family connection, these relationships can go far in helping a kid feel less excluded or isolated.

RELAY Critical Truths

God's Word is chock full of wisdom, insight, and admonitions about relationships. We know the most important and most satisfying relationship our teens will ever have is with God Himself. Whether they outwardly acknowledge that or not, I know from my experience that most teens want to believe that a Creator has a plan for their lives—that they are not meaningless objects in a vast cycle of life and death. Make sure your child hears that ***God made them to have a deep, abiding relationship with Him and to be a part of His great family.***

A couple of key verses offer wonderful support for this incredible truth. The first calls us God's friends: *No longer do I call you servants, for the servant does not know what his master is doing; but I have called you friends, for all that I have heard from my Father I have made known to you* (John 15:15). In other verses, if we have entered a relationship with God through Christ, we are considered His children: *See what kind of love the Father has given to us, that we should be called children of God; and so we are* (1 John 3:1). Just as family members can be like friends, so can we relate to the Father as both friend and child.

As adolescents begin to grow more aware of their need for belonging, many begin to disconnect from their church youth group. Although kids resist going to church for many reasons, some reasons are valid and understandable. Some kids tell me they stopped attending because they believed they'd outgrown their groups. Others say they had grown tired of feeling left out in a place where they should have been completely accepted. Some admitted they had veered away from their groups after making poor choices. When they tried to return, the judgment or ostracism they felt kept them away.

We must remember, however, that the church is more than youth activities. Being a part of the church doesn't mean that our kids should solely get to know other teens. Even if your kid isn't willing to attend age-graded groups, you can still encourage him to participate in other aspects of the life of the church. Find an avenue of service that lines up with his interests, gifts, or talents. If she is drawn to a specific population such as young children or the elderly, seek to connect her with adult volunteers. Help teens create intergenerational relationships in the greater family of God to get a sense of the diversity that lies within the church. Hopefully, these relationships can foster a deep sense of connectedness.

A second critical truth is this: *From the womb to the tomb, your soul will desire and require relationships in order to thrive.* The complexities of relationships are prevalent throughout God's Word. Stories about real people provide lessons on how to relate to one another, in good times and bad. When my daughter was in high school, her reflexive reaction to a particularly painful experience with friends was to push everyone away. While this temporarily protected her heart, we knew this would never satisfy her greater desire to be in fellowship with others. Isolation is the enemy of communion. And communion will always be a core desire.

Even though her connections at home regularly sustained her through difficult and lonely seasons, ignoring or overlooking this truth could have easily kept her from courageously stepping toward other people. As kids face the challenges that come through the presence or absence of connections, they need someone who will affirm their longing for fellowship while offering them wise words as they navigate rough seas.

The easy solution to a problem with creating or maintaining friendships is to reject or deny the need for community. The more difficult, yet more life-giving route, however, is to help our kids entrust their hearts to God as they attempt to find fellowship. He knows their longings well. On His timetable and in His manner, God can lead them toward people who provide them with friendship as they lean into Him.

Chapter 8

"Allow Me." I want to produce and be competent.

Work is so foundational to our makeup, in fact, that it is one of the few things we can take in significant doses without harm. Indeed, the Bible does not say we should work one day and rest six or that work and rest should be balanced evenly— but directs us to the opposite ratio. Leisure and pleasure are great goods, but we can take only so much of them.
— Tim Keller, Every Good Endeavor[1]

It is not that we are competent in ourselves to consider anything as coming from ourselves, but our competence is from God.
— 2 Corinthians 3:5 HCSB

When I first met Jared, he had just been expelled from high school. With no history of delinquent behavior, he surprised his peers and his family when he was caught setting off some small handmade explosives in the school bathroom. His bewildered mom was stunned, not only by his dangerous stunt but also by his overwhelming pride in his plan's success. However, he repeatedly denied that this was an act of revenge toward anyone or anything.

Instead, Jared kept saying he was just bored. With nothing to do after school and on the weekends, he often spent hours watching YouTube videos alone in his room. After watching several videos of kids setting off firecrackers or small explosives, he became obsessed with the idea of making them. He bragged about how quickly he learned to craft small explosives. Completely consumed by the process, Jared said he never considered the consequences.

Weeks later, Jared still expressed little regret. Despite the cost to his family, his school, and himself, he displayed a lingering pride over his ability to plan and carry out something so audacious. With too much time on his hands and no one to identify, develop, or direct his abilities, Jared's creation satisfied his core desire to be competent. Sadly, it also earned him a juvenile record and admission into an alternative school.

Jared's longing to be competent—though misdirected—stems from the positive directive God gave mankind to co-create with Him. In Genesis 1:28 when God commanded mankind to be *fruitful and multiply,* He was not referring solely to procreation. God was inviting us to partner with Him in producing something good and glorifying to Him. Together we were to care for His creation and for one another. In this way, the call to be fruitful refers to deeds (Prov. 12:11–14). A derivative of this same word is used in John 15:2 when Jesus directs His followers to stay connected to the vine in order to bear fruit—doing the work God has called us to do.

As adolescents move toward independence, a core desire to be productive should steadily emerge as well. Without an invitation to utilize abilities and resources in a productive manner, many kids don't know what to do to satisfy this often hidden yearning. They are bored, aimless, and unaware of how their interests, passions, or talents could bring about good for others, satisfaction for themselves, and glory to God.

Some of this confusion has occurred as societal shifts during the early part of the twentieth century powerfully changed our expectations of a teen's ability to contribute. Prior to this time, the word *adolescent,* as we know it today, did not exist. But a monumental manuscript written by psychologist G. Stanley Hall led to the popular use of the term *adolescent.*[2] This word broadly defined a period of development between childhood and adulthood that would ultimately change the American family.

As the Industrial Revolution caused hundreds and thousands of families to migrate from the farm to the city, older kids no longer had work on a farm to train and equip them for adulthood. Instead, they labored in factories. Once manufacturers developed more efficient and productive machinery, these new devices quickly replaced workers. Since the youngest were laid off first, more and more kids lost their jobs. In addition, the development of literacy campaigns, compulsory education laws, and child labor legislation allowed this age group to remain in school longer. Within a relatively short period of time, the number of kids who attended school beyond the age of twelve dramatically multiplied in the United States.

High schools were built to provide a separate place for adolescents to learn as they transitioned from childhood to adulthood. As a result, teens spent their time with others in this unique age group instead of with parents or other adults. Eventually, a separate culture of their own developed. With unique tastes and interests, the music, movie, food, and fashion industries began to cater to this subculture. Financially dependent on parents, they were not viewed as competent contributors to society. Instead, many perceived them as rebels who resisted societal norms as a way of exerting their independence and who consumed far more than they produced. Over time, many of these changes influenced cultural expectations concerning a teen's capability or competence.

Without a doubt, kids today are physically healthier, wealthier, and more resourceful than ever before. Yet due to these radical shifts in the perception of adolescents, our society expects less of them, especially with regard to their ability to contribute at home or in the community. Many believe Hall's term, combined with these major cultural changes, eventually cultivated this deficit view of adolescents as deviant, problematic, and incapable.

Robert Epstein, a psychologist and researcher, blames this interpretation for the gross infantilization of adolescents. His book *Teens 2.0* points to the many ways educational institutions and belief systems now presume teenagers to be incompetent and incapable. Epstein believes this viewpoint not only grossly stunts their growth and development but also robs them and our culture in many ways. He writes:

In most industrialized countries today teens are almost completely isolated from adults; they're immersed in 'teen culture,' required or urged to attend school until their late teens or well into their twenties, largely prohibited from or discouraged from working, and largely restricted, when they do work, to demeaning poorly-paid jobs.[3]

Epstein finds this completely ludicrous since his research reveals that thirty percent of teens are actually more competent than half the adult population across a wide range of abilities.[4]

The picture emerging from the science of adolescent neurobiology lends substantial support to his research. The proliferation and integration of neural pathways during this period in development leads to an increased ability for complex tasks. However, an adolescent's partially pruned brain, along with his increased attraction to risk taking, often overshadows his developing faculties. Since studies indicate that teens are likely to do something risky for the sake of reward or a temporary thrill, this neurobiological tendency can either aid or hinder them in their search to satisfy their desire to be capable.[5]

Nevertheless, with the right support and resources, teenagers can harness their brains' attraction to thrill by developing new skills, taking entrepreneurial risks, creating, discovering, and stepping beyond their comfort zones in order to gratify this core desire to be competent. Conversely, teens who are discouraged from doing anything outside of the norm or who are viewed as immature, incapable, or incompetent are being shielded from many satisfying experiences that can enable them to co-create with God.

Since God created them to partner with Him to bear fruit, then we must assume the enemy will do whatever he can to deter them and direct them toward destruction. He will use whatever it takes to arouse feelings of hopelessness, uselessness, or defeat to extinguish the flicker of motivation to be productive. Cultural norms, past failures, diagnostic labels, academic or behavioral shortcomings, low levels of confidence, comparisons to others, or other deficits will keep many from believing they can make a difference.

RECOGNIZE the Cry

Stories of adolescents doing remarkable things at school, in their communities, or around the world serve as powerful reminders that teens really do have the ability to contribute. While these kids may appear exceptional, more often than not, they have simply been required or encouraged to utilize what's been given to them.

Parents and caring adults play a key role in helping teens discover and redirect this oftenoverlooked desire within them. Note how the adolescents you know shield or display their heart's cry to be productive. Although your kid may not verbalize this desire, the longing exists. Some channel it well while others are still trying to figure out what to do with this often misunderstood or misidentified need to feel competent and capable.

Producing, performing, or creating through school-related pursuits

Extended years in school have no doubt given our kids a built-in arena in which to exercise this core desire. As classes become more demanding, many kids naturally satisfy this longing by completing their classwork. Homework, projects, and tests offer the opportunity to demonstrate competence. Apart from academics, most schools also offer various other outlets such as sports teams, orchestra, band, theatre, chorus, student government, and dozens of clubs or organizations.

These experiences not only tap into our kids' increasing abilities, they also give them a sense of confidence that can foster a vision for their futures.

The kid who accepts a challenge, or bravely enters a competition, or remains steadfast while working toward a goal begins to believe in himself. From these moments, God begins to weave a vision for their futures— and perhaps even a lifelong calling.

Being good at doing no good

Boredom, or the lack of purpose, quite often provokes kids to look for something to do. Their innate longing to produce, along with the excitement accompanying risk taking, leads them to direct their abilities toward the wrong activities. Jared represents a kid whose gifts and talents were unrecognized and therefore unharnessed. Having little to no vision for how his focus, determination, and ability to meticulously create something could benefit himself or others, he directed his energy toward a futile and dangerous endeavor. The last I heard of Jared, he had been arrested again and eventually dropped out of school.

Dr. David Elkind, the author of the acclaimed book *The Hurried Child,* describes how exhaustion and burnout has led many overscheduled children to disengage from extracurricular activities by the time they reach adolescence. Yet, at this point in development teens actually benefit from having a reasonably full plate. Not only does their productivity satisfy this emerging core desire, it also keeps them from directing their energy toward more destructive endeavors. Otherwise, they are at risk for being really good at something that is no good.

Allowing past difficulties to shape beliefs about competence

During their teen years, kids who chronically struggle academically and have little interest in athletic or extracurricular pursuits can easily believe they have nothing to offer. They attach competence to traditional activities. As a result, the kid who frequently naps, watches movies, plays video games, or scrolls through posts, pics, or products may not believe he has much to offer. He might complain, *every time I try to do anything, I mess it up! So, why try?* Repeated failures, negative experiences, and constant criticism can create a paralyzing fear that keeps many from ever stepping out of their comfort zones.

Although educational institutions may seemingly perpetuate this idea, adolescents don't have to be academically bright, athletically talented, musically inclined, or natural leaders to create, produce, or contribute. But if a kid isn't encouraged or required to participate in some way, many will waste time and do nothing. Lack of productivity or purpose is often linked to feelings of depression, loneliness, irritability, and anger. Regardless of whether these emotions are evident or not, idle teens will eventually feel restless and unsatisfied when nothing meaningful is connected to this longing.

Checking out by using substances

When teenagers don't know what to do with the relentless angst that arises when longings are left unmet, many will look for something to quiet the clamor. A common method of drowning or denying emptiness is to use alcohol or illegal substances. Almost every kid I counsel who abuses drugs or alcohol links feelings of boredom to their decision to use. Having nothing better to do, they push the envelope and try something new.

The risk involved, especially in the beginning, offers a feeling of excitement and adventure that they were missing. This same feeling could have come from healthy and more productive challenges. In my work with teens, those who are active and productive are less likely to use substances. Many don't feel the need nor do they have the time.

Apart from the behaviors mentioned above, this cry of the heart can be vague or subtle for many reasons. We may think that if a kid really wanted to be productive, then she would happily do what is required of her on a daily basis. Unfortunately, doing chores or completing homework doesn't always leave kids feeling gratified. Furthermore, because cultural expectations of adolescents are so low, many kids and parents overlook this longing altogether. In sessions, many kids share that they do nothing because not much is really required of them. Conversely, those who are out making a difference typically believe they were expected to do so and capable of producing and participating in some form or fashion.

RESPOND in a Helpful Manner

By the time our kids reach adolescence, most have something that gets them excited. This feeling may be related to a difficulty they have had to overcome. Usually, it's related to a specific topic of personal interest. When these passions are identified, affirmed, and linked to possibilities, development of competence inevitably blooms.

Adults play a vital role in prompting, encouraging, supporting, and even expecting our kids to do what they can where they are. One hundred years ago, passivity and idleness weren't tolerated. We can play a powerful role in turning the tide around by refusing to buy into the deficit view of adolescence. Here are a few ways that adults can facilitate this often hidden desire to contribute.

Point out the gifts, talents, and passions you see in them.

Adolescents often hear more about their shortcomings or weaknesses than about their gifts, talents, or abilities. Being reminded of past failures or repeated struggles can easily fuel defeating thoughts about their ability to do anything of value. Sometimes, a teacher, a parent, or another adult unknowingly reinforces their deficiencies through cutting comments, unreasonable expectations, or constant comparisons. Before you know it, beliefs about their own potential are squelched.

Taking time to point out strengths, especially when teens are struggling to find purpose, can help silence the constant critic that resides in each mind. Let them know what you see. Remind them of the positive observations and opinions of others. Discuss the many ways these skills and traits can be used to bless others. By regularly inviting them to dream about how they can contribute today as well as in the future, we echo the Father's heartbeat for His kids. Our words of encouragement about the gifts and resources they already have can empower them to look ahead at the many possibilities to co-create with Him.

Require your kids to contribute around the house.

"Never do for a child what a child can do for himself," a wise graduate professor firmly declared to our developmental psychology class. Once I had kids, I never forgot this advice. I wholeheartedly expected my children to do what they could at any given age. Set this expectation well before they reach adolescence. If they can make their lunch, let them make it. If they can load a dishwasher, or mow a lawn, or make their bed, then these should be expected of them. Why? Because these contributions give them a sense of being able to pitch in while also keeping the entitlement beast at bay.

Stay at home moms often tell me they feel guilty for making their kids do things around the house since they are home full time. One of the most important tasks for all parents is to work themselves out of a job. When parents stop infantilizing their kids, the children develop a sense of capability as they progressively increase their skillsets by doing whatever they can.

As adults, if you can do household repairs or a little plumbing, or plant a garden, or enjoy crafting, ask your kids to work alongside you. Not only can they gain some confidence as they assimilate these or other specialized skills, time together can build and strengthen your bond. Friends of ours have required each of their five sons and daughters to help their father build a small car during their middle and high school years. To keep them from losing interest, they aren't permitted to get their driver's license until the car is completely finished! This challenging project became a rite of passage for each child. They all encountered different challenges—and at least one openly proclaims how much he hates car repairs— but each gained a measure of perseverance and many practical skills.

Use assessments.

For those kids whose talents or gifts are more difficult to identify, an assessment offers a helpful perspective on their strengths. Popular inventories like *Strengths-Finder 2.0* and *Career Direct* give adolescents a comprehensive profile that describes personal preferences and links them to potential careers. These analyses do more than list future possibilities. They help them see a broad snapshot of their strengths and capabilities. They also help them recognize the value in their unique wiring. This can be especially helpful for kids who are very different from their siblings or parents.

Parents or caring adults will find profiles greatly aid them in motivating, planting seeds, and encouraging exploration. They can also lead to connecting conversations with other people who hold similar gifts and talents. Completing assessments is another way of showing kids that God has indeed gifted them in a way that will both satisfy them and bring glory to Him.

Discourage activities chosen solely for the sake of the college resume.
I often hear teenagers talk about what they should do in high school based on how it looks on a college application. For example, many join a club, run for office, or participate in a community activity to list it on their resumes. As someone who interviews applicants for a highly competitive college, I find an obvious difference between those kids who are genuinely engaged in an activity versus those who are constructing a billboard ad for themselves. Those who try different things or end up starting or pursuing something because of an inner passion or conviction have allowed experiences to refine and direct them. These kids are interesting and stand out far more than those who have tried to fit a mold or appear a certain way.

While many people, including guidance counselors, offer advice, remember that these years at home are critical to helping teens understand and explore how God has wired and equipped them. Placing a mold upon them is an easy way to squelch the plan He has for them. Instead, we can encourage them to take risks while also being good stewards of the gifts and resources they've been given.

Josh and Brett Harris had parents who encouraged them to do all they could as kids. Believing that many of their peers lacked the inspiration to do great things, they began a movement called *The Rebelution*. Their website (www.therebelution.com) is filled with stories about teenagers who are engaged in remarkable projects around the world. These teenagers all found something that ignited a passion and motivated them to do something in the area of activism, adventure, business, entertainment, faith, politics, science, and technology. Their stories should remind us that deep within every teen are both the desire and ability to do something for the kingdom.

Require older teens to work and/or volunteer.
Working or volunteering is a great way for a teen to develop a new skill or make a contribution. As your kids' privileges increase, so should their responsibilities. With getting a cellphone, driving privileges, later curfews, or other freedoms come the expectation that they will financially contribute, regularly pitch in more at home, and/or increasingly engage in the community at large.

When our oldest son turned sixteen, his fears about finding a job led him to devise many excuses for why he shouldn't work. When we recognized that his reasons had more to do with his anxiety about how to proceed, my husband helped him take the first step. He drove the car from one retail outlet to the next and gave him a pep talk before he walked inside. Soon he got a job. After two years of working at a neighborhood drugstore, this son talks openly about the benefits of being employed during high school. The managers loved his enthusiasm and hard work, and he loved being a part of something separate from our world.

When our daughter's unique schedule prohibited her from seeking traditional forms of employment, she started a cupcake business to give her more flexible hours. Her extremely profitable little venture allowed her to learn about many aspects of running a business while also providing her with the finances needed to pay for ballet related expenses. She also used some of the money to provide scholarships for a few kids who couldn't pay for lessons. When she left for college, she handed her business off to another ballet student who still runs it to this day. Both of our kids credit their work experience with giving them the courage and confidence to step beyond their comfort zones.

In many ways, parents may find it much easier to do everything for their kids. By completing tasks ourselves, we can certainly avoid arguments and the pitfalls of having to teach and re-teach them. We can also work to fund everything they need and never make them contribute financially. We can tell them what we think they should pursue in life and shield them from the struggle that inevitably comes when they have to figure life out on their own.

But what will any of this produce? I'm pretty sure it will only lead to the development of overly dependent, demanding, entitled, and fearful young adults who secretly wonder why they are here. In my opinion, we have too many aimlessly wandering around already.

RELAY Critical Truths

Like every other desire, the longing to produce has been distorted by mankind's fall into sin. In his book *Every Good Endeavor*, Tim Keller writes, "Without the gospel of Jesus, we will have to toil not for the joy of serving others, nor the satisfaction of a job well done, but to make a name for ourselves."[6] The ordinary and extraordinary work of our lives must be viewed in the context of God's command to produce—to co-create for the benefit of the community and the glory of God. The mundane tasks we require from our kids are the building blocks that allow them to understand this call. The work they accomplish in the areas where they contribute offers them great purpose while also bringing Him great honor. In a culture that convinces our kids to believe that their resources and the fruit they bear belong solely to them, we must take every opportunity to help relay the following two foundational truths.

First, our kids need to know that *an individual's abilities, gifts, talents, and resources come from God and are meant for Him.* (See Jas 1:17). Recall the scripture at the beginning of this chapter. Our sufficiency is from God (2 Cor. 3:5). God has given each of our kids unique bents and abilities for His great purposes. He desires that they be good stewards of His gifts (1 Pet. 4:10). While the work of their hands will often bless them, all work is meant to remind us of His goodness and grace. Ultimately, the mundane and marvelous tasks of the day offer yet another avenue of worship.

Recall the admonition God gave the Israelites in Deuteronomy 8:17–18. Once they had cultivated the promised land and seen the fruit of their hard work, God knew it would be tempting to take full credit for what they produced instead of recognizing His goodness. He said, *"You may say to yourself, 'My power and the strength of my hands have produced this wealth for me.' But, remember the Lord your God, for it is he who gives you the ability to produce wealth, and so confirms his covenant, which he swore to your ancestors, as it is today."*

He gave our kids many different resources. Whether they appear naturally bright, hardworking, kind, relational, witty, or artistic—all of these traits ultimately resulted from His original and creative handiwork.

The second critical truth they need to hear is that *God will direct their paths and supply their needs for whatever He calls them to do.* Allow your kids to regularly experience this truth in situations in which they must lean on Him. Rescuing them robs teens from seeing God as sufficient. They must face situations where their weaknesses, fears, and limitations cause them to look toward the One who is able to see them through. Not only can these *not enough* moments yield humility but also they can expand their awareness of their perpetual need for community.

God is enough, and He will always give them what they need to accomplish His will. *And my God will supply every need of yours according to his riches in glory in Christ Jesus,* writes Paul in his letter to the church at Philippi (Phil. 4:19). The only way they will produce lasting fruit that will greatly satisfy this desire to co-create is to stay connected to Him as branches to a vine (John 15:4–5).

Our kids have a core desire to do something that is meaningful, helpful, productive, and satisfying because God placed in them this longing to work with Him. As they move through adolescence, our willingness to help them water dreams, discover potential, and seek out opportunities plays a vital role in enabling them to live the abundant life to which God is calling them.

Chapter 9

"Touch Me." I desire and require physical contact.

To touch is to give life.
— Michelangelo

My soul clings to you;
your right hand upholds me.
— Psalm 63:8

In my almost three decades as a counselor, one young girl stands out as a grave example of the importance of touch. Her extreme story and her pain powerfully remind us of what a teen may tolerate in order to get what she deeply desires.

Chloe was twelve years old and had been placed in the custody of the state after someone noticed she had been living with an unrelated seventy-two-year-old man. It took days to find her drug-addicted parents. Before she met this older man, Chloe often wandered her neighborhood unsupervised for hours or days at a time. Although her parents sometimes left enough food for her, Chloe deeply needed touch and human interaction. This older neighbor regularly checked in on her and even offered to buy a few basic necessities when she needed them. Soon he became her faithful companion. Because of his seemingly genuine affection, she never questioned his intentions when their relationship became sexual.

Upon placement in a group home, Chloe was found to be four months pregnant. She had been told he was exploiting her; however, she fiercely defended him. "We hardly ever had sex," she exclaimed. "He really cared for me and made me laugh," Chloe sobbed as she desperately tried to explain their relationship and justify his behavior. In her lonely and deprived world, this man had regularly offered her both physical and emotional nurturance. Although his behavior was despicable and illegal, Chloe could only see his willingness to satisfy a physical and emotional connection she had unknowingly craved for so long.

The end of this relationship brought her intense feelings of anxiety and depression. Though it was difficult for me and the other members of the treatment team to hear her talk so lovingly about this disturbed older man, we understood. In all her young years, he might have been the only person whose touch reminded her that she was alive.

When God created a companion for Adam, he hardwired each of them with a deep, ongoing need for physical touch. Feelings of pleasure and wholeness now depended in part on the physical presence of the other. The Creator had declared the nurturing touch of another human being as *good*. When we lovingly offer and receive physical contact, our hearts recognize it as good.

Ideally, our first earthly experience with touch begins at birth when we are held in the arms of a primary caregiver. It continues until we are cared for by loved ones as we face death. We now know how and why these interactions are critical to our well-being. Research into touch deprivation has given us a plethora of evidence to substantiate the importance of touch.[1] From Harry Harlow's famous experiments in the 1950s on maternal deprivation in rhesus monkeys to current studies being conducted at research centers like The Touch Institute, we have learned the soul flourishes when exposed to healthy, nurturing touch and suffers, decays, and begins to die when touch is either abusive or absent.

From a physiological perspective, we can understand the basic reason. After healthy human contact, the chemicals released in the brain and body actually enhance overall health and human development. When our kids are touched in a nurturing manner, skin receptors beneath the skin send signals that cause the hormone oxytocin to be released. Oxytocin is also called the *bonding* or *cuddle* hormone because of the role it plays in deepening the connection between individuals.

The presence of oxytocin also lowers blood pressure, heart rate, and the amount of cortisol, or stress hormone, in the blood. Since too much cortisol can actually impede proper development while wreaking havoc on every physiological system, we can see why touch is so important during the adolescent years. Especially because adolescents often experience conflict, stress, and division with friends and family members, touch can provide reassurance and relief during a season in life that can be so overwhelming. When words are inadequate or off-putting, a warm embrace, a touch to the hand, a back rub, a pat on the back, or a stroke on the arm can communicate so much while satisfying a deep, never-ending longing within our kids.

Despite the obvious scriptural and overwhelming scientific evidence, many parents begin to withdraw physically once their kids display or express feeling awkward about parental touch. Other parents worry that regardless of how much or little physical affection they offer, their teen will inevitably seek to satisfy this core desire solely through peer relationships. Many parents I meet are resigned to the fact that these encounters will most likely involve promiscuity. Some fathers, uncomfortable with their daughters budding sexuality, back away from all forms of physical touch.

Any and all of these postures stifle a parent's willingness to proactively address our kids' need for touch. When they aren't offered a model for healthy touch during adolescence, they may not learn to distinguish between sexual touch and loving touch.

RECOGNIZE the Cry

Since adolescents are detaching from primary caregivers, most will indeed lean on peers to quiet this longing for touch. You can see this interaction where kids congregate: hugging, patting backs, slapping fives, sitting closely or on top of each other, holding hands, or kissing. Girls play with each other's hair while guys pat, slap, or even body slam one another.

Years ago, when my husband was on staff with Young Life, he would say the ideal place for the weekly club gathering should be seventy-five percent smaller than what we think we need. When kids are jam packed in a room while doing something fun, they are more likely to feel connected. These bonds are strengthened over time as bursts of oxytocin are released each time they gather.

Despite the many benefits that come from this kind of touch, other harmful interactions drive this desire as well. Caring adults should regularly monitor how this longing is being met or unmet at home and with peers. Several of the most common ways teens satisfy this cry in their peer communities are listed below.

Participating in athletics, team sports, group performances, or competition

The kind of physical contact kids receive through athletics and certain group activities can be very positive. Here, they huddle, stack hands, high five, aggressively slap arms, shoulders, or rears, and even body slam one another. If the context is healthy, the chemical benefits exist as well. In fact, a study of NBA teams was conducted recently to determine if touch somehow influences outcomes. After thoroughly studying the factors, they found that teams who displayed early season touch significantly correlated with increased cooperation and the overall success of the team.[2]

These findings shouldn't surprise those who have personally felt the social and emotional benefits of working closely with others toward a common goal. The cohesiveness of the group and the encouragement members experience through touch clearly affects each player's individual contribution.

Engaging in affectionate or sexual touch with same or opposite sex peers

Hormones, combined with curiosity and desire for physical contact, make it tough to resist the temptations of engaging in a host of sexual behaviors. Those kids who are touch starved at home and/or with peers are at increased risk of satisfying this craving through sexual touch. Adolescents engage in premarital sex for many reasons. There is little difference in numbers between Christian and non-Christian young adults. In a recent study conducted by The National Campaign to Prevent Teen and Unplanned Pregnancy, eighty-eight percent of unmarried young adults (18-29) are having sex while eighty percent who self-identify as evangelical say they have had sex.[3]

Of those I have counseled, both male and female—without exception—agreed that at some level, their decision to engage in sexual behavior was linked to a deep longing to be loved through touch. When these relationships come to an end, many grieve the physical isolation just as much as the end of the relationship—particularly those whose touch needs were rarely satisfied outside of the relationship. When the breakup happens, the powerful loss can overwhelm them.

This great hunger for touch may possibly explain why *hooking up* or having *friends with benefits* has been normalized among many young adults. By viewing these sexual encounters as a way of helping out a person in need, many young people rationalize their one-night stands or uncommitted relationships as satisfying their deep longing for touch.

Sexual touch isn't just happening between opposite sexes. Increasingly, adolescents are experimenting with sexual touch with same sex peers. When these kids find themselves experiencing pleasure, many begin to question their sexual orientation. "If it felt good," they say, "then this must indicate something about my sexual identity, right?" So many are allowing experimental behaviors and strong cultural messages to determine how they define themselves sexually.

Our sexually tolerant culture has certainly played a role in promoting this way of relating. From spontaneous kisses to sensuous physical interactions between members of the same sex, expectations and standards for sexual behavior have radically shifted in a brief amount of time. Without anyone to challenge these models, our kids will just mindlessly mimic the majority.

Watching pornographic material

Sexual images and videos are readily accessible for any age group. According to one survey, thirty-two percent of teens admit to intentionally accessing nude or pornographic content online.[4] By the time they are eighteen years of age, approximately ninety-three percent of males and sixty-two percent of girls have viewed pornography.[5] Even though pornography is repeatedly correlated with increased violence, sexual addictions, and sexual and marital problems, roughly two-thirds of young men (67%) and one half of young women (49%) still view pornography as acceptable. [6]

Moreover, according to the National Coalition for the Protection of Children and Families, forty-seven percent of families in the United States reported problems with pornography in their homes.[7] One survey reports that Christians view pornography just as much as non-Christians. By viewing and vicariously engaging in sexual activity, they satisfy touch needs and sexual desire. Unfortunately, the chemical released in the brain while viewing porn (dopamine) activates reward circuitry, which in turn makes breaking the habit more difficult. More intense scenarios and extreme acts are required to experience the same benefit. Over time, these pornographic images begin to shape how a person satisfies this core desire for touch while negatively impacting sexual norms.

Engaging in aggressive or violent touch

When compared to other nations, the United States ranks lower in showing physical affection toward adults or children. James Prescott, a researcher at the National Institutes of Health, reports that insufficient physical touch may actually be one of the reasons for the high levels of violence in the United States.[8] In the United States homicide actually ranks in the top three leading causes of death for people who are in the 10-24 age group.[9]

Although violence cannot be blamed solely on touch deprivation, nevertheless, touch deprived kids are stressed out kids. And stressed kids will find something to relieve their cortisol levels. One recent study demonstrated how healthy touch through regular massages actually reduced acting out behavior in delinquent teens when compared to those teens who only received relaxation training.[10] Massages, along with other forms of nurturing touch, significantly reduce cortisol levels. Without safe relationships and an understanding of the benefits of nurturing touch, adolescents may veer toward aggressive behaviors as a means of dealing with stress hormones while attempting to satisfy this core desire.

Because habits get harder to break over time, helping our kids find comfortable and healthy ways to cope with this longing for touch is essential. As you begin to recognize how your teens may be dealing with their need for touch, allow your observations to ignite a caring and empowering response.

RESPOND in a Helpful Manner

Virginia Satir, a renowned family therapist, once said, "We need four hugs a day for survival. We need eight hugs a day for maintenance. We need twelve hugs a day for growth."[11] While few adolescents lean on their moms and dads for those twelve hugs, a parent-child relationship offers a kid one of the safest and most meaningful places to receive touch. Although they are maturing, the sensations they received from primary caregivers actually remain embedded in their minds as they grow and develop. At a cellular level, our hugs or pats actually remind them and reassure them of the ongoing connection we still have with them.

Touch kids in a way that is mutually comfortable.
Because they are separating from us, unspoken fears make us wary of the possibility of crossing a boundary. We feel awkward. They feel awkward. Thus, our call as mature and caring adults is to take the lead in discussing and responding to their touch needs in a way that respects each kid's individual preferences.

Like a good reporter, tune into the what, where, when, and how regarding your kids' touch needs. Listen to what they say about current or past experiences with touch and be observant of current preferences. For example, instead of defending Aunt Lucy's intrusive methods of expressing her affection, allow these comments to help you glean information about what is comfortable to them. With a changing body and mind, expect this desire to alter over time.

Every adolescent is different. Recently, a father and daughter I know talked about how she leans into him when they watch television or chill on the couch together. Outside of that, she is extremely resistant to much affection other than a side hug. One of my kids is typically receptive to a hug or pat on the back from anyone, anywhere. Our daughter willingly engages with close friends or us but quickly pulls away. We know her stress levels are higher when she hangs on a bit longer or leans on us while lounging around the house. We call our third child a cat. Sometimes, he offers and receives hugs freely. Other days, you might as well hug a telephone pole.

Just because one child has been openly affectionate during childhood doesn't mean he will remain that way with Mom and Dad. Conversely, the kid who seemed independent and even physically distant at a young age may want and need parents to express their affection toward him in a way that respects his space but offers comfort. Whenever this conversation surfaces in counseling sessions, kids repeatedly remark that as long as personal preferences are considered, they are open to their parent's desire to touch them in loving ways. If and when they reject or resist your touch, give them space, and try again later.

Talk about the importance of setting physical and sexual boundaries.
Never assume an adolescent knows or understands why, how, where, or when to set physical and sexu-

al limits with others. Otherwise, their peers, movies, or their own spontaneous desires will set their standards. Research reveals that youth whose parents talk about the importance of setting physical boundaries were significantly more likely to remain abstinent than peers whose parents did not bring it up.[12]

Many well-intentioned teens simply believe a desire or commitment to make good decisions is enough. They can't imagine the many scenarios that can put them at risk for sexual promiscuity, let alone sexual violence. Their sense of invulnerability, along with their ignorance, sets them up to be ill-equipped when such situations arise.

Be the adult who will openly talk with them in a non-threatening manner about personal boundaries. Educate them on the way pleasure—and fear—can quickly and easily cloud anyone's good judgment. Otherwise, we leave them to learn from their mistakes. Although experience can be a great teacher, the many possible bad consequences should compel us to be proactive about the knowledge they need and how preplanned responses can impact their decisions.

I meet many girls, in particular, who say they first gave in to the sexual requests of their boyfriends because they felt badly for them. For example, she wrongly believed that since her presence contributed to his powerful sexual urges and physical discomfort, then resisting his request was equivalent to inflicting pain. While he might be uncomfortable, if he can appropriately manage feelings of anger or rage, he can certainly manage sexual desires, as well.

Furthermore, many kids believe that flirtation, plus sexual desire, somehow gives them permission to manipulate and control another person. As a result, if they experience sexual desire (or provoke these in another person), then they have no other option but to travel down a one-way road that ends with a sexual act they may not have planned.

In many ways conversations about the importance of managing sexual desire are no different than those we have with a toddler who throws a toy or a temper tantrum when she is angry. We set clear boundaries and teach her that intense feelings can be handled in better ways. Since all intense emotions are activated in the same region of the brain, the same self-regulation skills (removing oneself, breathing deeply, cardio activity, finding distractions, and so on) can actually be used to cool the sexual activation occurring in the brain and body.

When teens hang out in your home, clarify boundaries and expectations.
Encouraging your adolescent to invite friends over can be a positive way to strengthen social connections. Whether you are hosting their dates or their athletic team, be wise about the places and spaces in which they gather. While blankets, throws, and low lights can seem cozy and comfy while teens gather to watch movies, these create opportunities to cross

boundaries with one another. Surging hormones, emerging desires for touch, a lack of supervision, and an inviting setting—these can maximize temptation and set them up for failure.

Instead, make your presence known while still offering them some privacy. Most don't come over with the desire to cross boundaries. A few safeguards can keep them from heading down that road. If and when they are getting a little too close for comfort, kindly, yet directly, ask them to sit up and/or create more space between them. I don't think many parents realize how much most kids respect adults who maintain firm boundaries. Everyone needs someone who is a little stronger where we are struggling or still growing. With less accountability and no plan, however, crossing boundaries becomes more of an option, especially for kids craving touch.

Apply Wi-Fi safeguards at home. Regularly talk about pornography.

I have frequently heard the Internet being compared to Pandora's box. Through this incredible invention, our kids have access both to everything wonderful and everything evil. While we cannot completely protect our kids from being exposed to pornographic images, because this problem gravely impacts the hardwiring of their brains, installing safeguards at home and on our kids' devices is too easy not to do.

Explain to your kids the relational and physiological consequences of visually and sexually stimulating themselves through porn. Because dopamine, a neurotransmitter in the brain associated with reward circuitry, is released during this kind of stimulation, the brain begins to quickly crave more and more of the same. Over time the feelings of pleasure or the perceived reward offered will no longer be experienced unless images and/or encounters become more erotic or perverted. We now know that this process mirrors the cycle of addiction that occurs with other highly addictive drugs. As a result, addictions to pornography in men and women are on the rise.

The ongoing conversation needs to occur for many other reasons as well. Besides its addictive nature, pornography is abusive, denigrating to women and men, and destroys marital intimacy. Around the globe pornography is one of the most common problems couples face, impacting a partner's expectations and profoundly inhibiting their ability to experience sexual pleasure within the context of a healthy, sexual relationship. Few, if any, will hear these warnings from their friends, teachers, or pastors. They need a courageous adult who will continually talk about this massive problem in order to avoid facing the serious consequences that come from this seemingly harmless activity.

Encourage healthy methods of stimulating touch needs. When my kids began leaving for college, my husband and I decided we needed to get a puppy—aka transition object—to help us both cope with the loss. Dogs don't leave you until they die. Even though our kids were excited about this purchase, we never expected to see how much our friendly, fluffy pet would benefit them, as well. Our cute mini-golden is pretty hard to resist. Each of our kids used her to satisfy their longing for physical affection. Hardly an hour would go by when someone wasn't stroking, holding, or snuggling with her. Recently, while walking around with Bailey like a baby in his arms, one of my sons said, "I'm not going to lie. This dog majorly satisfies my touch needs."

Apart from safe, human contact, nothing is as comforting as a pet. Not surprisingly, furry creatures are being used in nursing homes, treatment centers, and even colleges to help combat stress and loneliness. Animals can decrease the presence of stress hormones while simultaneously satisfying the desire to be touched.

For those teens craving touch or whose love language may be physical touch, stuffed animals, soft throws, weighted blankets, hot showers or baths, and therapeutic massages can also curb our kids craving for touch. Each of these stimulates skin receptors in a way that mirrors some of the benefits of human touch. I often wonder if the huge success of the Snuggie came from a touch-deprived nation that feels a little relief from a blanket that basically envelops them. Whatever the case, items like these will remain popular because of the way they can take the edge off of a person's desire for touch.

Perhaps more than any of the eight desires, the cry for touch comes from a proven, physiological need. Research continues to reveal a vast array of positive outcomes when humans experience regular physical contact in the context of safe and loving relationships.

RELAY Critical Truths

Whether feeling stressed or depressed, dispirited or delighted, most adolescents will physically reach for trustworthy people to comfort, encourage, or celebrate with them. Brief or extended physical contact can certainly ease their burdens while strengthening a bond. But if healthy relationships simply don't exist or trustworthy confidantes are not accessible, our kids need to hear that their Creator is always available to them.

God doesn't reach down from the heavens and offer them a physical hug. But by His Spirit, He has the power to touch them in a manner that far surpasses any of the emotional and physical benefits of human touch. Because of this truth, every kid needs to hear two central ways that our God satisfies their longing to feel His presence.

First, because God formed them, teens are the product of His loving touch. As the Master Potter, he created and shaped them in just the way He imagined they should be. Even though they can't physically touch Him, what they see in the mirror—their physical appearance—comes from His creative imagination. They were fashioned by the same Creator whose mind and hands formed everything else in the universe.

When Jesus walked the earth, His physical dealings with people offer us a reflection of God's desire to intimately interact with us. In fact, in the Gospels alone, the words hands, fingers, and touch are mentioned nearly 200 times. Jesus touched a leper and took the hand of a woman while he healed them (Matt. 8:3, 8:15). He laid His hands on a blind man (Matt. 9:29). When Peter was sinking, Jesus reached out His hand and took hold of him (Matt. 14:31). When little children were brought to Him, He placed His hands on them to pray (Matt. 19:13–15).

The power of God to heal, restore, or bless did not require Him to touch. But knowing how physical contact can communicate love for another, Jesus assured them of His presence while acknowledging theirs through touch. These small yet meaningful gestures also demonstrated His willingness to enter their world of pain, suffering, and even celebration.

Although Jesus now resides at the right hand of the Father, before He left this earth He sent His Holy Spirit. While we may have preferred His physical presence, the opposite is truly best for us. Because the Spirit indwells the believer, God can touch every ounce of our being. This kind of supernatural touch far outweighs any comfort a human will ever receive from another.

When waves of peace overpower anxiety, when healing eradicates disease, or when comfort sustains us through painful situations, we experience His powerful presence. Our kids ultimately crave this kind of touch, especially through trials and tribulations.

Our kids also need to know that the Church is called to be the hands and feet of Christ. When a friend randomly shows up and sits with them in their pain, or a teacher embraces them, or a parent strokes their arms—these are portions of His provision being offered through a community of people. Having designed them for relationships, He knows what they need from others. When they cry out to Him in their loneliness, frustration, or fear, His presence can be felt in the form of caring souls who lovingly reach out to them. When loving hands are extended toward them, they're reminded of their beauty, worth, and significance. We're like Christ when we minister in these ways.

This need for loving touch represents one of the reasons why abusive touch or the lack of touch can be so damaging to the souls of our kids. When they're physically neglected or wounded by touch, our kids may internalize the lie that they are ugly, unworthy, invisible, or insignificant. A lifetime of believing this lie leads to isolation and eventually emotional death. Science has proven this is essentially what occurs when we are touch deprived.

We have a powerful role to play in the lives of our kids regarding this core desire. While it begins the day they are born, the physical interactions we have with them must continue, even if they look different over time. Our God calls us to reflect Him. We would do well to explore Jesus' examples of loving inter-actions and mirror the kind of touch that reassures, comforts, and heals.

Chapter 10

"Protect Me!" I long to be safe.

God does not remove us from all harm; He uses harm to move us close to Him.
— Dillon Burroughs, *Hunger No More Devotional*[1]

He who dwells in the shelter of the Most High
will abide in the shadow of the Almighty.
I will say to the LORD, "My refuge and my fortress,
my God, in whom I trust."
Psalm 91:1-2

William was a friendly, easy going sixteen-year-old from an upper middle-class family. He was one of the most likeable kids I have ever met. In the nicest way possible, he made sure I knew that counseling wasn't going to change anything. He went on to deny that he had any problems and used much of our first session to place more focus on his overprotective and irrational parents.

William contended that he'd outgrown the need for curfews as well as consequences. Because he excelled academically, he felt entitled to unlimited freedom. According to him, most of his friends' parents had long since given their kids' *carte blanche* control over their lives. His parents, however, reported that the more he was allowed to exert his independence, the more he made poor choices. In the past month, he had either come home high, intoxicated, or well beyond his curfew.

As his parents continued to communicate and enforce their guidelines, William became more angry and resistant. "I'm not a bad kid. If they would just let me be with my friends, then everything would be fine," he insisted, trying his best to keep me at a distance from his heart.

Over time, his growing frustrations led him to talk more about his seemingly picture-perfect all-American family. Although he knew I was aware of his dad's ongoing battle with alcoholism, when I had initially brought up this subject, he'd discounted the problem. He also adamantly denied that his dad's addiction impacted him at all. Now that his parents had expressed concern over William's habits, he willingly shifted the focus to his dad's addiction. In doing so, he was finally able to verbalize the effect his dad's drinking had had on him throughout his childhood.

As a youngster William often withdrew to his room when his dad appeared to be out of control. As he got older, he felt more annoyed than frightened. Every time his dad reached for a drink, the tension became palpable. To avoid the stress, William spent as much time as he could with friends and less time at home. Not having to see, hear, or wonder whether his dad was drunk shielded him from the unpredictability of his dad's addiction.

Even though his dad had been sober for a year, William still hung out with friends as much as possible. More time with them meant their choices or habits heavily influenced his. When a few of his buddies began to experiment with drugs and alcohol, he followed suit. Eventually, his friendships—combined with the relief he felt using substances—became the perfect refuge. The very threat of losing either one provoked major feelings of anxiety.

In a world full of emotional and physical threats, home should ideally be a completely safe place. For many kids, family problems make them feel unsafe, threatened, or insecure. Some of these problems involve addictions, domestic violence, marital problems, sibling conflict, blended family issues, constant arguments, and financial strains. To cope with the stress, kids devise ways to feel safe and shielded from the possibility of harm.

Even if a kid grows up in a relatively safe environment, he will eventually face a social, emotional, or physical threat in some arena of his life. This world is broken. On this side of heaven, we will never experience complete peace. In fact, though we crave it, we can hardly imagine a completely safe environment.

Adam and Eve experienced safety in the garden. There they felt harmony and peace. When they gave in to temptation, disobeyed God, and ate the forbidden fruit, their environment abruptly shifted. As sin and death entered the world, their survival depended on their ability to shield themselves from harm.

We inherited a brain and body that has been wired for protection. Designed to scan continually for danger, the brain and body experience a whole cavalcade of physiological events. If a kid perceives something or someone as emotionally or physically unsafe, in an instant, the body is ready to attack or avoid the culprit—the well-known "fight or flight" reaction. Even if no detectable threat exists, stress hormones will flood his brain and body. These chemicals lead to an increased heart rate, shallow breathing, hypervigilant eyes, an upset stomach, and digestive issues. All of these are associated with feeling anxious or afraid.

The more anxiety, stress, and insecurity they experience, the more teens will long for their heart core desire for safety. By the time kids approach adolescence, this longing will prompt them to search for people, possessions, or behaviors that seem to offer them the security they crave.

RECOGNIZE the Cry

Whether intentional or not, parents, relatives, friends, and even best friends will say or do something that provokes fearful thoughts and feelings within teens. In an effort to reestablish a sense of security, kids will automatically move away from the unsafe person or situation and toward the people or places that appear to offer the best protection. If these relationships aren't available or don't exist, many will settle for someone or something that offers the illusion of safety.

Although coping patterns vary, adolescents often try to satisfy this core desire for protection in four ways. The presence of any or all of these patterns of coping may be an indication that they perceive a threat and feel insecure.

Escaping or withdrawing to a bedroom, a friend's house, or another location

For many kids their bedrooms offer a safe haven in their houses, especially when life is stressful. Extended periods of solitude protect them from the constant commands, corrections, or criticisms they receive from siblings and/or parents. Others automatically retreat when a particular person or situation is present.

Removing oneself from a stressor can be a healthy and non-confrontational way of shielding oneself from pain. But the adolescent who frequently disappears or completely disengages from the family for long periods of time may be doing so to shield himself from being attacked or threatened in some way.

To escape the unpredictability or insecurity of home, many adolescents would rather lean into their relationships away from home. Hanging out in the neighborhood, seeking extended hours in school or work settings, wandering the streets, or moving from one friend's house to another—these are a few common ways adolescents seek safety from others.

While an adolescent's desire to be with friends is healthy and expected, when they resist balancing this time away with time at home, they may be purposefully running from a threat or stressor. Because these planned or spontaneous disappearances are rarely accompanied by words, parents and caring adults can reasonably infer these actions indicate they are trying to find something or someone to satisfy their heart core desire for safety.

Maintaining a defensive or aggressive stance toward others

With a rapidly growing and changing brain still far from being mature and fully integrated, an adolescent's increased awareness of social and emotional threats can cause him to overreact by defensively or aggressively responding to even the slightest stressor. As if a major threat to homeland security has occurred, some kids can seemingly move from low level to severe level within seconds. The teen that continually remains in a defensive posture may have learned that putting down her guard might place her in a vulnerable position. Past wounding or shaming experiences have taught her that she must remain alert to potential attacks or hurt. For some kids, this defensive stance is the only way they know how to interact with others, even though it can isolate them as well.

Sometimes, kids who remain *on guard* are pegged as having an anger management problem. Any kid who grows up in an environment where social, emotional, or physical threats never seem to subside will no doubt project feelings of anger. Sadly, the kid who uses anger to cope often pushes away people and possibilities that may offer him the safety he desires.

Many teens have been exposed to unending abuse, rage, and chaos. Trusting another person enough to put down their weapons (so to speak) feels completely unnatural and deeply frightening. The brain remembers the rejection, humiliation, shame, or abuse. With a body designed to recognize and respond to anything that might simulate or even provoke these memories, kids will find it hard to shift out of this protective stance into a vulnerable one until a long period of safety and trust has been established or re-established.

Self-medicating to ease the fear, anxiety, or stress
Teens need to experience long periods of rest, renewal, and relief from feeling threatened. Otherwise, the stress hormones that continually circulate through their bodies will eventually wreak havoc on every major bodily system. Over time, gastric problems, headaches, muscle pain, or difficulty focusing—along with feelings of anxiety and depression—may never fully subside. In their efforts to relieve some of the discomfort, many kids begin using medications to address individual symptoms. While drugs often pro-

vide temporary relief, unless the source of the stress is addressed, the discomfort will eventually return.

As a result, kids who can't escape from relationships or situations that pose some kind of perceived or real threat are at an increased risk of using illegal substances to ease the pain. When they experience intense pleasure or relief and find they can easily forget their worries, many will return for more. For those in a home full of uncontrollable conflict or chaos, this habit numbs the pain and offers an escape from their reality. Unfortunately, using substances moves them closer to other forms of danger while moving them farther from healthy people and relationships that can offer them the safety they crave. This pattern also leads to addiction.

Self-harming to deal with bullying or abusive behaviors
According to the National Center for Education Statistics, approximately twenty-two percent of adolescents have reported being bullied in some form.[2] These acts of aggression include antagonistic behaviors like punching, hitting, smacking, teasing, voicing threats, using sexually derogatory terms or labels, isolating, excluding, humiliating, and/or spreading rumors. While kids cope with this kind of abuse in different ways, one study in the *Journal of the American Academy of Child and Adolescent Psychiatry* indicated that kids who were bullied during childhood are much more likely to engage in self-harming behaviors during their adolescent years compared to those who were never bullied.[3]

These behaviors include anything that causes them to harm their bodies such as cutting, head banging, ripping skin, or punching oneself. Although self-harm can be linked to many different causes, some kids do it for the same reasons that others self-medicate. They are trying to numb or alleviate intense, discomforting feelings associated with feeling vulnerable. Self-abuse becomes their way of coping with the pain and stress that endure long after words or actions end.

A sincere effort to understand teens' coping patterns, along with commitment to advocate for their safety, can provide a bit of the peace God intended for our kids.

RESPOND in a Helpful Manner

When kids are young, they openly express feelings of fear or insecurity to parents and other adults. As they approach adolescence, however, most begin to disguise these discomforting feelings. The thought of being perceived as weak, dependent, or unable to protect themselves makes it very difficult for teens to be open, honest, or vulnerable.

We may see them as strong, independent, and mature adolescents. Underneath that façade may be a kid who has worked hard to hide her feelings and protect her heart from feeling exposed. Because of this pattern, my suggested responses are really more rules to live by.

Commit to being a "safe" adult.

As a family, maintain a variety of healthy relationships. Safe people can help our kids identify unsafe people. Encourage your kids to freely talk with friends, mentors, or other safe adults about their relationships. Having open conversations with others can provide a safety net of people who can help identify risks. In the event that something or someone threatens them, most teens will run toward those people who have proven to be safe and who appear committed to protecting those who aren't.

Emotionally and physically safe people respect the rights of others, even when provoked. They don't violate these in order to gain power or control. They commit to communicating their thoughts and feelings using words and a tone that does not threaten, belittle, wound, or shame. They avoid emotional or physical threats of any kind. They also maintain control by refusing to touch or inflict physical harm, even if their emotions intensify.

Safe adults are role models for teens to be emotionally and physically safe themselves. Admittedly, modeling is easier said than done. Financial challenges, marital difficulties, work-related stressors, health problems, relational strains, and a myriad of other difficulties can make it difficult to keep us from unraveling. Add a strong-willed, rebellious, opinionated adolescent in the mix, and our commitment to modeling can easily fly out the window. When we fail, our willingness to admit wrongdoing and ask for forgiveness goes far in reestablishing a safe relationship.

Refuse to discount reports of any kind of abuse, even if the perpetrator is a family member or close friend.
Many parents don't realize how seemingly benign words, actions, attitudes, and behaviors may be perceived as threatening. To us some words or actions may not appear to be a big deal; however, the hurting person may have felt genuinely threatened. Instead of dismissing the possibility that a well-meaning person is unsafe, we should note kids' behavioral patterns and engage them in dialogue about what people or places arouse feelings of fear and insecurity.

Regardless of whether the threat is coming from a parent, sibling, relative, coach, teacher, or peer, we must work hard to advocate for their safety. Never assume you know the intentions of the perpetrator by saying things such as "He didn't mean that." If we defend the aggressor and don't affirm the experience of the one who is wounded, she may begin to discount or dismiss her gut responses, eventually permitting others to rule over or violate her in some way.

Even though adolescents can certainly exaggerate some details while omitting others, we must be willing to patiently listen and seek to validate their perspective. Allow kids to share their stories so that they can make sense of their experiences. Even if their accusations are incorrect or misguided, the feelings that accompany these are rarely concocted. A chronically stressed or fearful teen is experiencing something that threatens his safety.

Also consider the way you respond to emotional, physical, or sexually abusive actions or intentions. Yelling, verbal attacks, constant arguments, shaming behaviors, taunting, constant threats, and unpredictable behaviors—especially related to addictions—occur in millions of homes everyday. When we allow these behaviors to continue, and we do nothing to discuss or address them, we may be perceived as unsafe as well. If we choose to make light of them, overlook, dismiss, or even deny their presence—for whatever reasons—we indirectly perpetuate the threat. Not only that, we teach teens that the behavior is acceptable and should be tolerated.

Communicate boundaries and consistently follow through with consequences.

In many ways an adolescent parallels the toddler who fearlessly tries to tread beyond his boundaries. He needs authority figures that will lovingly and firmly communicate appropriate limits. Though outwardly resistant, adolescents deeply respect and gravitate toward adults who are committed to protecting them, especially when they aren't willing or able to do it themselves. When parents don't set boundaries at all—or worse yet—overlook a boundary crossing, teenagers often believe they're not worthy of protection. I have heard many teens say, with a hint of sadness in their eyes, "They really don't care what I do!"

Recently, I counseled a high school student whose parents discovered that she'd been repeatedly sneaking out and drinking. She was shocked when all they did was lecture her. She begged me to tell her parents to ground her and make her stay home. Knowing she didn't have the emotional strength to say *no* to her friends, she desperately wanted her parents to set the boundary. When parents set rules and guidelines, they help their teens develop the capacity to set their own, as well. This training will help them deal with the demands and risks they will inevitably encounter throughout life.

How do you know if a boundary is clear? First, a teen must be able to easily identify and articulate a boundary. It can be written or stated but needs to expressly communicate what is and is not allowed. Second, ask your teens to confirm what they read or heard by having them tell you what they understood. Third, make sure you clearly express what the consequences are for violating the boundary. These need to be in proportion and relevance to the transgression.

When we follow through with the consequences, we have no need to yell, put down, whine, or revisit past problems. Instead, announce what will happen and remain as calm as possible. An emotionally or physically volatile parent communicates that they can't handle their kid's transgressions. Afterward, if you must, find a safe friend who will let you vent, complain, or even freak out in front of them. I love how John Townsend expresses the importance of boundaries in his book, *Boundaries with Teens.*

> Kids will run up against your decision 10,000 times. Your job is to hold the line 10,001 times. Take a deep breath, pray, call your friends and hold that line. God made parents to be the guardrails on the twisting road of life. You need to be strong enough for kids to crash into over and over and over again. You must stay strong, so that your teens will learn to stay on track. Guardrails get dinged up. But if they work well, they preserve the young lives that run up against them."[4]

Use local, national, and global problems/trends as a springboard for discussions about threats.

In our world close to twenty-one million adults and children are bought and sold into sexual servitude or forced labor. Abuse and prejudice against minorities and vulnerable populations continues to exist. Women are marginalized, demeaned, and sexually objectified. Pornographic images set sexual norms. Our kids can easily become desensitized to the gravity of abuse. We can't grow indifferent. We must discuss these issues with our kids.

These subtle and overt forms of emotional, physical, and sexual abuse grieve our God. Our Creator weeps at the way people use and abuse others in order to gain power and control. Our kids must see our sorrow and concern. They must also see what we do to bring about change. By praying together, donating to a cause, or actively participating, our kids learn to take a stand, speak up, and act appropriately toward others.

Our young men need to know it's never acceptable to harm, take advantage of, or compromise the safety of any human being. By refusing to tolerate any form of abuse, they not only reflect the heartbeat of their Creator, they courageously make a powerful statement to their peers. When a teenage boy tells his teammates in the locker room to stop mocking or humiliating a girl or woman, he protects the safety of another human being. Openly standing against anything abusive strengthens his moral and spiritual fibers while honoring God as well.

Discuss the signs and symptoms of toxic and unsafe dating relationships.

Surveys indicate that at least a third of all high school students have been or will be involved in a verbally, emotionally, physically, or sexually abusive relationship. Despite this reality, only thirty-three percent of teens who are in an abusive relationship tell anyone.[5] Too often, they fear what may happen if they speak up. Before your kids enter a dating relationship, talk about typical behaviors associated with unsafe relationships.

Toxic partners may try to control the other person, make irrational accusations and threats, use isolation tactics to cut off support systems, pressure them to engage in unwanted activities, humiliate, or degrade them. They may have explosive tempers. Sometimes, adolescents stay in these relationships because they feel controlled by the other person. They cope by remaining passive. Other times, they simply don't know what it looks like to set healthy boundaries.

Some kids believe that saying *no* or setting boundaries within a relationship sounds unkind or mistrusting of the other. Instead, it demonstrates dignity and self-respect. It leads to understanding how they can satisfy their desire for safety while in relationships.

Kids can be taught to use code words or secret phrases that can be verbally communicated or texted when they perceive danger. Many apps are now available that allow the user to quickly and easily communicate with a preselected group of people where they are and what they are doing, especially if they feel vulnerable or in danger. *Circleof6* and *bSafe* are two that remain popular.

Though we are fallen, imperfect people who can never completely protect our kids, we have been called to shepherd them. A shepherd creates a safe area and sets boundaries to protect his sheep from predators. He scans the area around them for looming threats. If something endangers their well-being, he does not overlook, dismiss, or minimize it. Instead, he responds by addressing the threat so that the sheep are safe and learn to recognize the presence of danger. By so doing, the shepherd reflects the heart of the Great Shepherd.

RELAY Critical Truths

While I certainly don't pray that my kids will experience harm, I know that God uses their fears to draw them closer to Him. He wants them to personally experience the relief that comes when we *abide in the shadow of the Almighty* (Ps. 91:1). Even the safest place, plan, or person pales in comparison to the protection that comes from an all wise, all-knowing, and all-powerful God. As you regularly live out your calling as a disciple, be intentional about relaying these two powerful nuggets of truth that let teens know how He deeply satisfies this heart core desire for protection.

The first is that our **God promises to be a safe place, a refuge, a shelter in the storm.** Regardless of our circumstances, we can lean into Him. Psalms 46:1–2 reads,

> God is our refuge and strength,
> a very present help in trouble.
> Therefore we will not fear.

He provides us with the specific help we need and a peace that we can never create on our own.

During a thirty-day backpacking trip in Wyoming, our daughter Emily experienced this powerful truth when she found herself in harm's way. After falling behind from their projected course, her crew ended up above the tree line just as a fierce storm was brewing. When heavy rains descended and lightning struck closer than she'd ever seen, everyone immediately fell into lightning position. With her body in fetal position and her face between her knees, she began to cry, as she feared for her life.

Desperate to experience peace, she began thinking, then saying, and even shouting truths of Scripture while begging God to protect her. She told us that within just a few minutes, her praying turned into singing. With an incredibly calm spirit, she began to pray for those around her, her family back home, and for His perfect plan to unfold. Even though Emily had certainly been afraid at other times in her life, she had never experienced this kind of danger. Years later, she still says she's grateful she got to experience God's overwhelming presence and peace in the midst of an inescapable storm.

We can tell our kids all day long about the incredible peace available to them through God. Let your teens hear that and see how you personally model this truth. As you battle fears, talk openly about your choice to lean into Him for protection. However, an explanation or even a personal testimony can't completely capture the overwhelming presence and peace that God offers. God hears His people when they cry out to Him. While He may not choose to deliver them from the threats, His ability to protect and preserve His people far surpasses anything or anyone a mortal can offer or create.

Even adolescents who have a personal relationship with God may seek something apart from Him to satisfy their need for safety and security. Not until they personally experience the limitations that exist in every man-made provision will they seek the comfort and safety of His wings. We must lovingly remind them that God will draw near to them as they draw near to Him (Jas. 4:8). His limitless ability to protect His people in accordance with His plan is the ultimate satisfaction for this core desire.

The second truth related to this longing is that *the center of His will is always the safest path to take.* Corrie ten Boom, who endured the Holocaust, once said, "There are no 'ifs' in God's world. And no places that are safer than other places. The center of His will is our only safety—let us pray that we may always know it!"[6] As adolescents face various social, emotional, or physical threats, they will certainly struggle to figure out what to do and where to go. There will always be the path of least resistance, as well as the one with the most. Some will lead to unsafe places or unhealthy people. Others may seem benign but may oppose biblical principles, leading them toward destruction and away from God. Only a God who knows everything and who cares about everyone can promise the perfect path.

We must emphasize the importance of remaining obedient to His commands and His leading even when threats or difficulties encompass them. As they seek Him with their whole hearts, He will allay their fears as He leads them through myriad difficulties. The God who overcame death, the greatest foe we face, is able to defeat and overpower any person or power that may appear to threaten them.

When our kids were younger, we rarely watched the news with them. Worried about how headlines might affect them, we shielded them from hearing any disturbing news. As they got older, we used these stories to help them understand the problems of the world. We also reminded them that Earth is not our home.

Because wars, acts of terrorism, mass murders, racial discord, violence, and all forms of evil will never completely subside until Christ returns, point their eyes heavenward. In a world where threats exist from every direction, they long to experience the kind of peace and security that only He can offer by His Spirit and through His Word. Each of us who have a personal relationship with Jesus can rejoice, knowing that *he who is in you is greater than he who is in the world* (1 John 4:4). He is alive and at work—a very present help when we are in trouble.

Chapter 11

"Remember me."
I yearn to impact others.

"Everyone will be forgotten, nothing we do will make any difference, and all good endeavours, even the best, will come to naught. Unless there is God. If the God of the Bible exists, and there is a True Reality beneath and behind this one, and this life is not the only life, then every good endeavour, even the simplest ones, pursued in response to God's calling, can matter forever."
— Timothy Keller, *Every Good Endeavor*[1]

O Lord, make me know my end
and what is the measure of my days;
let me know how fleeting I am!
— Psalm 39:4

Emotionally distraught teens slowly streamed out of the funeral service. Long embraces, tearful outbreaks, shell-shocked expressions, and staggering gaits openly displayed the pain they felt over the sudden death of their beloved friend, Chase.

"I can't believe he's gone," lamented the girl sitting behind me.

"I was just hanging out and laughing with him a few days ago," responded her friend.

For the next few weeks, thoughts about Chase dominated conversations in our small town. Some focused on unfolding details about the wreck. Others wondered how this tragedy would impact those who knew and loved him. All were struggling to absorb the permanency— the sting—of his death.

To honor him, several of his closest friends placed a large wooden cross and some chairs near the site of the wreck. Here they could gather, place notes or memorabilia, and grieve together. Being reminded of their own human vulnerability and mortality seemed to strengthen their bonds with one another. Recognizing that death's disruption could happen to any one of them, those I knew began to consider their reasons for living—their ultimate purposes or callings in life.

Losses like these lead kids to contemplate deep philosophical and spiritual questions for the first time. Why am I here? What do I want to accomplish before I die? How do I want to be remembered? Perhaps God uses these shocking realities to let us know how fleeting life is (Ps. 39:4). When God created us, He *set eternity* in the human heart (Eccl. 3:11 NIV). While His imprint may cause us to live fully and fearlessly, it also reminds us of the finality of death.

Teens' maturing cognitive abilities give them the capacity to reflect backward while simultaneously dreaming about the future. In other words, they can integrate the experiences of yesterday with those of today while thinking about tomorrow. They recognize the degree to which they can control the next chapters of their lives. Possibilities and dreams begin to ignite. They realize how they play a role in writing their own stories. This core desire to be remembered slowly emerges.

Many classic movies portray what American mythological researcher Joseph Campbell described as "the monomyth" or the "hero's journey."[2] He theorized that many of the most famous myths and stories from around the world share a similar structure. The hero's journey typically begins with a call to go on an adventure. Despite his initial reluctance, he rises to the challenge with the aid of an ally or powerful force of some kind. Once he enters the world of the unknown, he must face resistance and overcome a crisis. Upon his success, the hero is rewarded, and the world around him is forever transformed.

Popular movies like *Harry Potter, Star Wars, The Hunger Games, Lord of the Rings, The Lion King*, and *The Wizard of Oz* all contain this basic template. Perhaps these stories resonate powerfully with both adolescents and adults because they stir up an innate desire for adventure—for a calling uniquely their own. Kids become increasingly aware of the perils in the world around them. Here in the hidden corners of their hearts—as dilemmas, difficulties, and even death unfold around them—God awakens dreams and promotes purpose. Many begin to wonder how their abilities might be of use. As they dream, their personal quests or callings begin to form.

This heart core desire to be remembered is designed to drive them toward a God who wrote and orchestrated the greatest Hero's journey imaginable. Since He placed within them the yearning to impact others, He alone knows how their combinations of passions and abilities will meet the needs of this broken world. To bravely embark on the long and slow journey to discover God's unique quest for them will require time, effort, encouragement, and—most of all—courage.

Meanwhile, the noise of the world will challenge the very idea that one can have an eternal impact. Our kids will be attracted to the self- and pleasure-centered paths that offer the illusion of a legacy. The more they walk away from His plan for them, the more they threaten to mute the inner core of their souls—the place where this personal invitation to journey with God has long been brewing.

RECOGNIZE the Cry

With the ability to see the world in a whole new manner and a growing sense of their own competence and convictions, teens express thoughts and feelings about issues around them. Some of their ideas seem destructive and self-centered. Others are lofty and rather idealistic. All indicate a desire to have an impact, to leave a legacy, to be a part of something that lasts forever. Here are some signs that reveal to parents and caring adults that this heart cry longs to be validated.

Striving for popularity or notoriety

My jaw literally dropped while watching a documentary on the evolution of advertising. During a segment on the influence of social media, the interviewer spoke with a mom who regularly posted YouTube videos of her teenage daughter talking, singing, and dancing. As though they were experts on building a public platform, the mother and daughter relayed the importance of looking cute and sexy from head to toe in order to earn more *likes*.

When the interviewer asked why they spent so much time, money, and energy doing this every day, the mom eagerly explained that more *likes* meant more attention. More attention increased the possibility of more subscribers. More subscribers could help her videos go viral. And having a video go viral resembled obtaining the Holy Grail. A viral video could possibly lead to fame and fortune. With this incredibly shallow goal for her daughter, the mother hoped her teen would reap a reward from being recognized and remembered.

Caught up in the illusion that popularity or notoriety can somehow satisfy this core desire, many kids

191

(and parents) behave in a similar manner. The process or path may appear more sophisticated, socially acceptable, or intellectually challenging, but the underlying goal is often very much the same. In a world with few heroes and even fewer who are on a quest to bring glory to their Maker, we can hardly blame our kids for believing that being well known will somehow quiet this deep cry within them.

Leaving a legacy of diaries, blogs, videos, and selfies

A friend of mine sheepishly admits she kept a diary in high school so her biographers would have information on her early years. Although some teens have a stronger sense of wanting to be remembered than others, let's be honest. We long to think that someone, especially our loved ones, will want to comb through every photo and detail of our lives when we pass on. Even children ask, "Are you going to post that on Facebook?" (Which, as we all know, seems to have a shelf life of about a thousand years.)

Speaking out on culturally relevant causes or popular issues

This core desire to be remembered emerges in slow and subtle ways. We may first notice it through an adolescent's strong and often abrupt way of stating their perspective or opinion. Recently, a teen client criticized a friend who had announced his choice of a college and a major. In an arrogant tone he remarked, "I don't know what in the world he was thinking!"

I could have responded—and it would have been quite natural for me—by defending his friend. Instead, I let his fervor fuel a conversation about his passions, interests, and dreams. Eventually, it became clear that the cutting comment about his friend was actually an indicator. He desired to make an impact in a very different way.

According to researchers who study generational trends, millennials tend to be more civic, progressive, and politically engaged than other age groups. Due to the accessibility of media, we have all become more aware of cultural trends and recent events. As a result, any breaking news in the community or across the globe can quickly prompt an online conversation. While instant access has many benefits, these passionate discussions can sometimes fuel a bandwagon response. Although many adolescents are well informed on an array of issues, their naiveté combines easily with their impulsivity. Some passionately adopt the popular view without full knowledge of what they've agreed with.

This situation happened recently when our state voted on a controversial social issue. Many followers on one of my daughter's social media feeds instantly began to express strong opposition. The idea of contributing to a huge and complicated discussion influenced her to join in and agree. Within twenty-four hours, it appeared almost all of her online *friends* felt exactly the same way.

For the person whose heart is looking for a cause or quest to get behind, a teen is vulnerable to supporting national movements without full consideration of all the facts. Impulsively joining the outspoken majority can quickly satisfy this desire to leave a mark while leading teens to ignore previously held principles or convictions.

Forming relationships to leave an impact

At this point in the book, it should come as no surprise that relationships play an enormous part in how heart core desires are satisfied. Even the loss of these relationships sparks an awareness of heart cries. Those who attended Chase's funeral listened to how his life impacted his friends and family. They heard his closest friends share stories, a poem, and even a song about how his life affected them. Not surprisingly, the legacy we leave is felt most by those who know us best.

Because adolescent peer groups tend to be such a central part of their lives, teens feel they have the most lasting impact through relationships. Here they already have a personality or alter ego that is often known only by close friends. These groups give them a place to try out character traits or personalities. As they begin to figure out who they are, they get closer to discovering how their gifts, talents, and abilities might make a lasting contribution to the world around them.

Unfortunately, teens may try to make an impact by trying to *fix* a friend or date. I have met many females (and males) who are dating someone because they believe they can make the other a better person. Seeing the person's great need or their potential to meet it, they can easily put aside the grave problems, risks, or challenges their behaviors pose for them. Their longing to be a hero keeps them from setting boundaries, letting go, or involving the help of someone more experienced.

Positioning themselves as a hero in romantic or close friendships can create patterns of codependence. Such attachments also increase the likelihood that they will engage in unhealthy behaviors. Since they feel so good about how they are helping, they may see things irrationally. While each of us hopes to impact friends and loved ones positively, an adolescent's limited resources, skills, and perspective often negate whatever good they may seek to do.

RESPOND in a Helpful Manner

Though it certainly requires a bit of restraint, we must slow down our automatic responses and really tune in to what a teen is saying or doing. Then we can help them explore how their heart core desire to impact others might be emerging. If we immediately attempt to rebuke or correct them, we may actually squelch or stifle this emerging core desire. As adolescents feel safe and heard, they will share their thoughts about the future.

Observe and discuss how talents, passions, and skills relate to calling.

By the time our kids enter high school, many of their innate abilities and passions have begun to surface. Over the years, participating in different activities has powerfully shaped their desires. Let them know what you see blooming inside them. You offer a perspective they don't have. These deliberate conversations about their giftedness can empower them to think and dream about how these may be utilized both now and in the future.

Often, when I mention an attribute I see in a kid (e.g. courage, advocacy, compassion, fearlessness, empathy, creativity), they're surprised. As I explain my perspective, they begin to put the pieces together and recognize how their unique stories have yielded this fruit in their lives. Conversations about career and calling can certainly induce stress for many adolescents. Inject these with the hope that comes from knowing that God is faithful to make their paths clear as they lean on Him. He promises to accomplish great things through them when they choose to resist the temptation to live a life that fosters personal gain instead of God's glory.

Give them space and permission to consider their life calling.

In order for kids to properly separate and individuate themselves from their family, we know that freedom, permission, and space should slowly increase as limits and boundaries decrease. In order to be open to God's call, parents and adults must mirror this principle as teens begin to consider different possibilities.

This process is harder than it seems. We often assume because we know them so well, we know what our kids should pursue academically or professionally. We also fall prey to the cultural expectations around us, especially when we have high performing kids.

Our kids certainly benefit from having parents and adults who will be sounding boards for them. We must be careful not to let our own desires or personal expectations squelch the process. Many kids fear their parents' rejection or disappointment if they choose something other than the expected route. If they don't feel they are allowed to do what they deeply desire, many will do what's expected instead. I've met many adolescents and adults who express great regret because they gave in to the pressure to conform.

While we may be spot on regarding what we think our teens should do, their relationship with and dependence on God can be greatly strengthened when we remove ourselves a bit from the wrestling ring. He may be leading them down an unexpected and unfamiliar path in order to accomplish what He desires in and through them. He invites them to be a part of His great adventure on this earth. Our own fears can greatly interfere with discovering how He's calling them to be remembered.

Expose them to people who obediently follow God's call.
Several years ago, we invited a missionary couple to
our house for dinner. As they talked about the mir-
acles they witnessed, as well as the challenges they
faced on the mission field, I watched my kids' expressions. They were completely mesmerized listening to
the stories this couple shared. After they left, one of
my kids wondered aloud whether God would ever
LET him be a missionary like them. Even though the
couple had in no way glamorized their work, our son
was drawn to what God can do through a servant
who obeys His call.

Our kids need to hear from Christians who have
travelled paths very different from the norm. Support
and invite those who are doing God's work into your
home. Watch biographical movies. Read books about
extraordinary men and women of God. Now that your
teens are older, include them in conversations with
your friends who are daily walking with the Lord.

Our kids need to get a sense of how God uses each
one of us differently in the places and spaces in which
we work and reside. These everyday conversations
about living out our daily call give them a powerful
glimpse of what this desire looks like on a daily basis.
Many times God has used these rather commonplace
conversations to teach my kids something about the
cost of wholeheartedly following God. He has also
graciously used these everyday exposures to whisper
dreams and visions to them about the future.

Encourage mission or volunteer work

Part of increasing their freedom and providing them space means we encourage them to engage in mission work in our communities and around the globe. Whether they volunteer in a tutoring program, harvest vegetables at a community garden, participate in a Vacation Bible School program, clean up highways, or help build housing—when adolescents volunteer, they experience this desire to impact others. These opportunities also shape their interest in a particular problem or people group. As they see the needs and contribute in some way, God faithfully uses these experiences to influence their personal calling or professional pursuits.

For the kid who has a hard time stepping out on their own, going on a family mission trip may help them feel more comfortable in the beginning. According to the Barna group, only eleven percent of American churchgoers have ever gone on a short or long-term mission trip.[3] A survey reported that the trip significantly changed their lives. They gained an awareness of poverty and injustices while increasing their compassion for those impacted. When teenagers have the opportunity to step beyond their comfort zones and serve people who are hurting or hungry for the gospel, many will gain a vision for the work that God can accomplish through them.

Be mindful of the legacy you are leaving.
One of the greatest and lasting legacies a parent can leave their children comes from their willingness to live out the call of Deuteronomy 6:5–7:

> *You shall love the Lord your God with all your heart and with all your soul and with all your might. And these words that I command you today shall be on your heart. You shall teach them diligently to your children, and shall talk of them when you sit in your house, and when you walk by the way, and when you lie down, and when you rise.*

As we personally walk the talk and daily obey God's commandments, we show them how to satisfy this longing to be remembered. They are watching us. They see when we choose to love the unlovable, befriend the friendless, or give to the needy instead of storing up treasures for ourselves. They see whether we extend mercy and grace to the undeserving. These actions demonstrate what it means to be a servant of a great God who works in and through His people. We give meaning to the verses and biblical truths they have heard at church and read in their Bibles. They gain a sense of what Micah 6:8 looks like: *to do justice, and to love kindness, and to walk humbly with your God.*

Our commitment to Christ means we are not our own and have been bought with a price (1 Cor. 6:19–20). Because we are His, we are here for His purposes: that His work and His kingdom might be remembered through a surrendered life. As we know by reading the stories of those who have preceded us in our faith, this path isn't without suffering. A calling from God doesn't prevent our teens from experiencing pain or persecution.

They will receive direct and indirect messages that counter this call: flashy façades, pricey possessions, and surface relationships. The Creator made them for so much more. Our kids were made for lives connected to the vine in order to bear eternal fruit. They hope you'll share your walk and your wisdom with them so they'll know what this looks like. Regardless, He lovingly promises His presence to sustain them when they seek Him with all their hearts.

RELAY Critical Truths

God calls His people to serve others, make an eternal impact, and humbly accomplish great things ... not for our kingdom or our glory but for His. Even though we know teens will be most satisfied when they are part of God's eternal work, their sin nature will continually lure them toward anything that brings glory to anyone or anything but God.

I often ask kids to take note of the *marbles* of this world. What do they really have to offer? Though shiny and attractive, they never fulfill forever. Obeying His commands and His call on their lives is the only path that brings eternal joy. To have a lasting legacy, nothing compares to the satisfaction of participating in God's kingdom work.

Because they're living on a battlefield, our kids need to know **the most impactful life comes from a willingness to be completely obedient to God.** For the kids who've made a commitment to Christ, they must recognize their role as chosen servants (John 15:16). If they don't have a personal relationship with God, then we must lovingly invite them to consider His invitation. This "monomyth" is no myth at all. Instead, it's their story within His-story. They're invited to partner with the Hero of all time in the greatest adventure possible.

This commitment doesn't excuse them from working hard to be the best at their studies, sports, and activities. Nor does it mean they sit around idly waiting for Him to call them into action. Instead, it means they choose to live lives fully surrendered to Him. Also let them know that no matter how we may plan, in the end the LORD establishes our steps (Prov. 16:9).

As these conversations occur, our kids need to hear **God remembers and rewards those who are obedient to His call.** In contrast to the shallow, self-focused, and often greedy role models that abound, the book of Hebrews offers us a list of people who were remembered because of their faith in God (see Heb. 11). Though the path they chose was uncommon and often wrought with pain, they left a legacy that still encourages millions of followers. These men and women made the choice to cling to God's plan even when the outcome was unclear. Their faithful devotion and willingness to be a servant of the Lord earned them an inheritance as their reward (Col. 3:23-24).

Believers who followed their lead provide a picture of how eternal consequences occur through ordinary people surrendered to God. Men such as Jonathon Edwards, George Whitefield, Charles Wesley, J. Hudson Taylor, Dwight L. Moody, Charles Spurgeon, Dietrich Bonhoeffer and Oswald Chambers come to mind. Women such as Teresa of Avila, Amy Carmichael, Frances Ridley Havergal, Joan of Arc, Catherine Booth, and Harriet Tubman also stand out in this believers' hall of fame. They left His mark on this earth as missionaries, evangelists, pastors, reformers, theologians, musicians, activists, and writers who cared more about furthering His kingdom than their own.

So that He might be famous, so that He might be glorified—these believers chose daily to be steadfast, faithful, and obedient. By doing so, each accomplished great works for God's glory while filling this deep heart cry to leave a legacy. Satisfying this core desire by surrendering oneself to the will of God isn't a message our kids will hear from most of their peers or from the media. If they never respond to the Greatest Story ever told, then the world's shallow and self-satisfying pursuits will overshadow this glorious call. They need your voice to help them imagine a life where God allows greater works to be done through them than even Christ was able to complete while on earth (John 14:12).

It can be tough to believe that God can do amazing works in an adolescent when we see them at their worst, weakest, and most resistant. I often pray that the Lord will give me glimpses of how He plans to use my kids for His glory. However, I find myself getting caught up in the dominant conversations between parents of teens—academic concerns, college preparation, relationship stressors, and so on—and can't see beyond today. I have to remind myself to keep praying for God's perfect will to be revealed to them and to our family.

Let's ask God to give us eyes to see them doing His work, wholeheartedly focused on bringing Him glory and honor and praise. Pray that in the midst of *a crooked and perverse generation,* they will *appear as lights in the world* (Phil. 2:15 NASB).

Section Three: The Paths of Desire

In Section One we focused on the complexity of the hidden heart as defined by Scripture. In Section Two we surveyed the eight heart core desires that God places within each of us. You read many examples and stories about how each of these can either direct kids toward God and community or toward destructive activities and disastrous relationships.

With the kids you know in mind, I hope you are now wondering why one kid chooses to go down a relatively harmless path in pursuit of desires while another can't seem to get off a path that repeatedly leads to pain and self-destruction. If you haven't thought about this yet, I invite you to ponder this thought for a bit.

Unfortunately, as teens seek to satisfy desires, no formula can keep them from taking a painful path. Perhaps we can see, even if they can't, the end result of their choices. We long for our kids to experience the abundant life that exists on this side of heaven. In this final section, we will explore three key factors that play the largest roles in how our kids live out their heart cries.

Pain and Protective Mechanisms

Chapter 12, "A Wounded Heart," will point out the ways that past and present pain shape the ways our kids seek to protect themselves. These protective mechanisms inevitably affect how they begin to automatically acknowledge and address heart core desires.

Sin, Self-rule, and Surrender

Chapter 13, "A Wayward Heart," follows the discussion of pain. Here we place the desires of the heart within the grand narrative of the Bible. Our sin nature leads to a mistrust of God and a desire for self-rule. The enemy lures our kids down three destructive paths that lead them away from God and community and toward self-ruin.

Traveler-Guides and Shining Examples

The final chapter of this section and of this book, "A Guiding Heart," emphasizes the importance of modeling the Great Shepherd. Our kids are relating to us, watching us, and wondering what we do with the eight desires that exist within our own hearts. By daily leaning into Him and applying the gospel to our own struggles, we offer a living example of what a vulnerable and yielded heart looks like in relationship with God and community.

Pain and protective mechanisms. Sin, self-rule, and surrender. Traveler-guides and shining examples of a trusting heart. Together, these forces play dominant roles in determining the paths our kids will choose as they deal with desires. I pray that God will use each chapter in this section to give you a measure of insight and wisdom as you seek to help the teens in your life understand the power and purpose of heart core desires.

Chapter 12

A Wounded Heart

The frequent attempt to conceal mental pain increases the burden: it is easier to say, "My tooth is aching," than to say, "My heart is broken."
— C.S. Lewis, *The Problem of Pain*[1]

He heals the brokenhearted and binds up their wounds.
Psalm 147:3

"Lady, if you think you can make me like, or even love, the man my mom wants to marry, you need to know that will never happen." Following her no-nonsense warning, seventeen-year-old Annie crossed her arms, furrowed her brow, and glared at her mom. "Just like every other man my mom dates or marries, Gary will leave her and us."

With that, she looked down at her feet and said little else. Because Annie had repeatedly threatened to leave home if and when this new husband moved in with them, her mother brought her to counseling. Unfortunately, the pain and confusion Annie had endured through repeated losses couldn't be resolved quickly. After the abandonment of her biological father during her early childhood, two divorces by step-fathers, and the recent, unexpected death of her maternal grandfather, Annie's unwillingness to accept another man in her mom's life made perfect sense. I couldn't blame her. Annie had no interest in signing up her heart for more hurt.

Despite her mother's physical presence during each loss, Annie felt alone through all of them. To Annie, her mother appeared more interested in finding another husband than being fully present with her little brother and her. She had tried to be good and kind, an easy kid, so the men her mom dated and married would stick around. Perhaps then she would have fulfilled her longing for emotional connection with a mom and dad. But after a decade and a half of seeing men come and go, Annie was tired of dealing with the loss of both her mom's attention and the men's presence. While she openly blamed and even ridiculed her mother for these failures, Annie privately believed she must be the real problem.

Unknowingly, Annie's pain affected the way she interacted with her peers. Using a combination of approach and avoidance strategies, Annie sometimes decided to do whatever it took to be everyone's friend. She became the person they wanted her to be and tolerated just about anything in order to protect herself from being alone. At other times, when these behaviors taxed or disappointed her, Annie avoided everyone. She convinced herself that people were stupid, and she was fine living as a loner.

Little did she know that the pain she endured throughout her childhood shaped the way she dealt with the desires of her heart. As Annie began to make sense of the way wounds had impacted every dimension of her soul, she connected the dots and slowly learned new ways to accept and address the emptiness she felt.

Pain Slices Across the Soul

Recall from Chapter 2 that the soul encompasses both the outer self (social and physical) and the inner self (mind and spirit). Living in a fallen world means painful experiences affect every aspect of the soul. Over time, kids develop coping mechanisms that shape the way they deal with the pain and emptiness associated with unmet heart core desires.

The brain and body remember physical pain in order to protect us. When kids experience emotional wounds, the resulting pain greatly resembles physical pain. However, you can't see the metaphorical bruises, cuts, or deep gashes that slash and injure the heart. For this reason, kids (and adults) are often unaware of how emotional wounds and their responses to them powerfully influence the way they react. If wounds remain unacknowledged or buried, their effect on how kids cope may never be connected to the wounds' emotional roots.

Even though the specific form and frequency of wounds varies, we group the most impactful wounds into four categories: loss/abandonment, rejection, humiliation/criticism, and betrayal. [2] If we add each category to the diagram used in Chapter 2, we can visually understand how these wounds literally slice across each layer of the soul, leaving their marks behind.

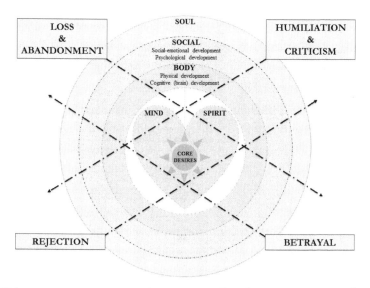

Diagram 5: Four Major Wounds Slicing Across the Soul

Most of us don't have to try very hard to remember an experience in each of these categories. Maybe the event happened over a short period of time, but its memory has had long-lasting effects. Our *behavior*, the way we now interact with others and with the world, has been influenced forever. Each of these events has changed the outer person, or the *social-phys-*

ical parts of us. Some changes may be recognizable such as numbness, nausea, tingly sensations, or muscle aches. Others cause cellular changes in our stress mechanisms that affect every system in the body.

Moving from the outer person to the inner person, social and emotional pain can mark the *mind* as well. Our bodies and brains are designed to remember and protect us. Our thoughts, beliefs, and emotions connected with the wound don't readily disappear. Finally, profound or repeated pain can leave an enduring scar on the *spirit* of a child, thereby affecting this deep place that influences her will, values, and overall conscience.

The soul, while incredibly complex and resilient, is also very vulnerable and easily wounded. Every person with whom a child interacts can bring his soul either hurt and despair or hope and healing. The people who have the most power to leave their marks on the soul are typically the closest, those who play a primary role in a kid's life.

This is a far cry from God's original plan for His people. In the garden, humans would never experience loss, abandonment, rejection, humiliation, or betrayal of any kind. In relationship with Him and with each other, they would share deep and lasting connections as they lovingly partnered with one another in the work they were doing with and for God. Being a part of God's family would have meant full inclusion, acceptance, and safety.

At best, on this side of heaven, our kids will only experience what C.S. Lewis describes as "good images of what we really desire ... the scent of a flower we have not found."[3] Even the best people, relationships, and groups will fall short. While it may seem depressing and unnecessary to dwell on this reality, knowing how wounds impact the soul equips us to understand pain. We can share this understanding with teens we shepherd.

Loss/Abandonment

Most kids have experienced some form of loss or abandonment well before their teen years. The death of a parent, grandparent, close relative, friend, neighbor, teacher, mentor, or pet can be considered a loss. Divorce, custodial changes, broken romances or friendships, geographical moves, or certain developmental transitions representing the end of a chapter or season of life powerfully provoke feelings of grief, sorrow, and even deep despair.

Another form of loss occurs when kids experience an overt or subtle emotional detachment, or passivity, from another person. Although this person appears to be physically present, the emotional connection that once was there has changed or disappeared. Many kids (and adults) struggle to connect their sense of loss with the pain or discomfort they feel.

When a parent is removed from the home due to domestic violence, abuse, or addictions, a kid may have difficulty recognizing and grieving the loss. Because the other parent may celebrate the renewed sense of safety, the child may suppress or repress his pain. Regardless of the type of loss or abandonment, letting go of a relationship that was or could have been satisfying doesn't come naturally. Adolescents may display a whole host of behaviors in an attempt to restore the connection.

Rejection

Similar to the pain of loss and abandonment, teens experience rejection. Rejection by a parent, stepparent, family member, teacher, coach, friend, or romantic interest typifies adolescence. Feeling excluded by others often provokes far more pain than grief from loss, especially when rejection is chronic or includes close relationships. When someone they value doesn't find them worthy or acceptable, kids question, suppress, or reject heart core desires in order to protect their souls from additional pain.

I have counseled many adolescents who heard someone significant say they aren't wanted, good enough, or acceptable in some way. Even if it came from a mere acquaintance, adolescents tend to take such remarks very personally, causing them to doubt their self-worth. A parent, close relative, sibling, teacher, coach, or best friend may have made a flippant comment. Or the message may have been repeatedly delivered through verbal or nonverbal messages. Rejection slices deeply across the soul.

Teens experience exclusion and rejection through silence in a group, lonely lunches, special classes, elite clubs, assigned groupings, designated levels, social cliques, and other perhaps well intended associations that may divide more than affirm.

While none of these may arise from malicious intent, the child or adolescent who is not accepted, included, invited, or sought after feels rejected. And prolonged feelings of rejection water feelings of shame, causing a kid to believe she is bad, broken, or unworthy. These beliefs or shame statements have the power to immobilize her when it comes to dealing with desires of the heart.

Humiliation / Criticism

Every kid enters the world with a deep and enduring desire to be known. When parts of the self are revealed, the response we all hope for is validation, affirmation, or perhaps even adoration. Thus, when kids experience humiliation or sharp criticism, mind and spirit recoil and remember.

Recently, I counseled a teen that recalled being bullied in her middle school years. Every day her stomach ached, her head pounded, and her heart hurt. Going to school was like entering a war zone where she was attacked by words, nonverbal gestures, and laughter about her weight, hair, complexion, clothing, and even her family. Eventually, she learned to blend into the background, hide herself and her voice, and thus avoid the possibility of attacks. Revealing any part of herself to anyone seemed to set her up for more pain.

Adolescents are beginning the process of separating and individuating. Receiving unkind, critical, and humiliating comments from peers, parents, or significant others can stifle the courage they require to become their own unique persons. Mean spirited remarks, mockery, scorn, sarcasm, rude gestures, condemnation, shaming, unfiltered and unkind judgments through put downs, bullying or cutting comments—all have the power to shape what a kid believes to be true about who they are, what they're doing, and where they're headed. As a result, the fear and shame these words instill powerfully affect how they cope with their heart core desires.

Betrayal

As a child grows and develops, interactions with others will inevitably lead to violations of trust. A friend he thought could keep a secret discloses information to others. Someone lies or distorts the truth. A trusted adult turns against her.

Depending on the depth of the relationship, betrayal can cause a child to withdraw the ability to trust anyone. The greatest damage occurs when betrayal comes from a primary caregiver or significant adult. These people are assumed to be safe havens, protectors, and comforters. While we would certainly include mothers and fathers in this category, we can also add close family members, teachers, youth workers, or other guiding adults. Ideally, these safe relationships allow children to be open, exposed, and vulnerable. In this position, they learn to make sense of the world. Dr. Dan Allender writes:

> Safety is the glue that allows the child to connect the different pieces of reality without fear or condemnation. When trust is tragically violated, it eventually causes a child to withdraw from learning and growing and causes suspicion of all caregivers, including God.[4]

When someone deemed safe violates a child emotionally, physically, and/or sexually—or the child sees someone else violated—intense betrayal results. This wound may also occur when a non-offending parent or adult caregiver does little or nothing to protect a child, even though s(he) is aware of the violation. The absence or breakdown of safety in primary relationships brings fear. This fear, or intense anxiety, causes a major shift to occur in the brain and body.

The stress response system makes it difficult to rest, relax, and trust others. Instead, the brain remains on guard, constantly assessing what other threats loom around it. Relationships once deemed safe now leave the kid feeling vulnerable and unprotected. If someone she trusted wounded her like this, then anyone can betray her. She may maintain a guarded (aggressive or over-reactive) or avoidant (timid) posture.

The heart's desire to be heard, noticed, affirmed, befriended, allowed, touched, protected, and remembered comes from a God who placed these within each of us. Every layer of the soul is designed to assess and respond to relationships. Key questions such as *Am I loved? Am I included? Am I accepted or affirmed? Am I safe?* help us determine whether to move forward or move on. Anything or anyone that threatens this possibility is remembered by our brains and bodies, which were designed to protect and preserve us.

When our kids experience any or all of these four wounds that run counter to these God-ordained desires, their hurt will cause them to form strategies to deal with the wounds. These behaviors arise to avoid the risk of more pain, to remain invulnerable, and ultimately to keep them from needing others.

Protecting the Heart

Over the years as a counselor, I have seen pain covered over, wrapped up, bundled, and shackled in many different ways. I have met kids like Annie who bear hidden wounds with friendly smiles and a servant-like nature and then at other times make sarcastic remarks and or behave destructively. I have met just as many who wear their pain on their sleeves, hoping others will respond to the constant flow of emotional "blood" spilling from them.

Because so many factors affect the way a kid copes with emotional pain, we can't predict why one appears rather resilient to the wounds of their earlier years and another can't seem to move beyond a single negative experience. People, perceptions, patterns of pain, personality, and many other protective or risk factors influence not only how each deals with pain but also how each copes with the relentless desires of the heart.

The wise parent or caring adult can best help by understanding the most frequent coping methods kids (and adults) utilize to deal with the four wounds.

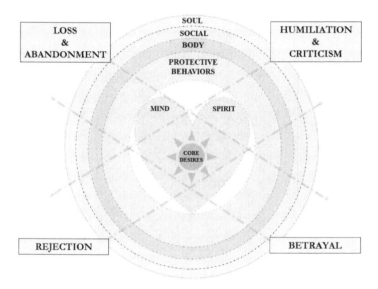

Diagram 6: Protecting the Heart

Building upon the diagram of the four major wounds in Diagram 5, I have depicted a wall of protection in Diagram 6. To prevent future wounds, children and adolescents guard the inner person, where the heart lies, by building protective attitudes and actions. These walls are conscious or subconscious attempts to keep them from feeling wounded, immobilized, and defenseless.

By engaging in defensive behaviors, they build an illusion that if they can cut off the negative thoughts, images, and emotions caused by the wounds, they will somehow avoid the pain. Unfortunately, because protective mechanisms create a barrier between the inner person (the heart) and the outer person (relationships and the physical body), these attempts actually cause a disintegration, or disconnection, within the soul. Disconnection leads to disharmony or inner turmoil. Instead of alleviating the distress and discomfort felt throughout the soul, the pain is inevitably perpetuated.

Moreover, even though the heart may be essentially cut off from the outer person, every aspect of it still bears the burden of pain. Trauma research has taught us a great deal about this phenomenon.

Traumatized people chronically feel unsafe inside their bodies: The past is alive in the form of gnawing interior discomfort. Their bodies are constantly bombarded by visceral warning signs, and, in an attempt to control these processes, they often become expert at ignoring their gut feelings and in numbing awareness of what is played out inside. They learn to hide from their [sic] selves.[5]

In order to avoid pain and keep themselves from feeling vulnerable and dependent upon others, kids will engage in protective mechanisms that can take many different forms. The most common include *denial, disconnection, destruction,* and *distractions.* While these can lead to a heart that is cut off from the rest of the soul, they can also create a temporary buffer that enables a kid to push through pain.

I often call *denial* the big cover-up. In order to preserve and protect themselves from more relational pain, kids will often play pretend. They will prop up a false front, appearing *together,* and denying any emotional or mental anguish. "I'm fine," "It's not a big deal," "I don't care," or "It didn't bother me"—each statement depicts an attempt to project an integrated and satisfied soul. When these kinds of responses follow a huge disappointment, you may assume they're only saying these things to keep others (and even themselves) from knowing the true state of their hearts. Denying the pain by pretending all is okay keeps them from having to deal with the debilitating thoughts and emotions that naturally begin to swell in the heart following a wound.

For short periods of time, denial can be helpful and may even shield them from more pain. Over time, however, denial never helps the heart heal. Instead, it buoys the fear that if they tune into the pain, they will be overcome, immobilized, and further trauma-tized. The opposite is actually true. By facing the pain and even exposing it to safe people, they can begin to make sense of the experience and begin to heal.

While denial is a verbal attempt to hide pain, *dis-connection* tends to involve behaviors. When relation-ships have yielded pain instead of pleasure, a child's automatic response may be to pull away. Hiding out in bedrooms, spending excessive amounts of time alone, and zoning out on video games, social me-dia, or other electronic devices may all be conscious or subconscious attempts to shield or protect their hearts. Although helpful in the short term, extend-ed periods of disconnection create a wedge between themselves and people who may be able to help.

If kids are humiliated or criticized when they display negative emotions, they may feel shamed. Shame fosters a tendency to disconnect in order to hide or suppress negative emotions, which may be viewed as a sign of weakness. Over time, this pattern of behavior can block the formation of intimacy since emotional honesty is a critical building block for authentic connection.

Alcohol and illegal substances are another com-mon means of disconnection among youth. Accord-ing to the National Institute of Drug Abuse (NIDA), people take drugs for a variety of reasons: 1) to feel good, 2) to feel better, 3) to do better, and 4) out of curiosity or because others are doing it.[6] With adoles-cent development in mind, we can understand how each of these may lure a kid to cope with their pain by using drugs.

Depending upon which substance they use, discomforting feelings can be replaced with relaxation, happiness, energy, or a sense of self-assurance. Feelings always remain tethered to thoughts. When new, more pleasant emotions arise, negative and intrusive thoughts, memories, or beliefs temporarily fade.

I can't think of one counselee whose drug use was not eventually linked to a method of dealing with pain and discomfort. Even if the teens didn't begin using to suppress pain, most quickly realize how the anesthetic or euphoric results of drug or alcohol can benefit them when stressful and/or painful feelings arise.

Sometimes, as kids search for strategies to cope with the hurts in their hearts, they end up hurting themselves even more. This is certainly the case with repeatedly leaning on disconnection through the use of substances to deal with pain. Substance abuse overlaps with other protective behaviors grouped in the category of *destruction*. Other destructive behaviors include self-injury, extreme thrill seeking, illegal activities, and promiscuity. They serve to provoke new emotions in order to cause others to subside. When kids experience a rush, intense pleasure, or even temporary relief as a result of these experiences, the possibility that they will reach for these behaviors again dramatically increases.

Other forms of destruction include aggressive words, attitudes, and actions meant to keep people far from their hearts. Filthy language, accusations, and harsh criticisms exemplify how this protective barrier can quickly create tension between a kid and someone else. Destructive actions can include behaviors that range from physically harming a person to destroying their possessions, property, or even their reputations. All of these are overt or covert attempts to cause pain in others that somehow mirror the agony or heartache within the adolescent.

Distraction, the final category of protective mechanisms, overlaps with each of the others. Similar to a form of denial, distraction is an attempt to cope with hurts by turning one's attention to something else, anything else. The kid who excessively busies himself or even obsesses over a relationship, an extracurricular activity, or academics may be doing so to avoid past or present pain. Because of the amount of affirmation associated with this method of coping, many kids continue to ignore their hearts as they overly focus on the activity that yields a great and visible reward. The kid striving for absolute perfection or becoming a workaholic may be doing so to attain acknowledgement, affirmation, connection, or affirmation. Because being busy will consume his time, energy, and mind, he can keep from tuning into the clamor of his heart.

In a similar way, the kid who moves from one activity to another, allowing little to no margin in between, may be doing whatever it takes to keep her mind from hearing negative messages as well. Consider our culture of kids who constantly wear headphones, scroll social media, and rarely sit alone in complete silence. In my estimation, these too can be attempts at distracting themselves from a hurting heart—a heart that fears it will never fully receive what it desires.

Although all of us will at times lean on protective mechanisms to protect our hearts, we run the risk of shielding our heart from the very things it desires. When we see these mechanisms appear, they should serve as reminders to us. First, they remind us that these were devised as a result of past or present pain.

Second, the behaviors may distract us from the root causes. If we concentrate on the mechanism being displayed, we won't keep probing their hearts, looking for clues behind the behavior. To do so, we must be safe and caring people with whom they can let down their guards. Only then do we have a chance at entering into the sacred spaces of their hearts. Herein lie desires entwined with a myriad of hurts and fears.

As we will see in the next chapter, the heart is also tangled up in sin. To shepherd this place in our kids requires a deep understanding of how their sinful natures will further shackle their hearts as they seek to satisfy desires.

Chapter 13

A Wayward Heart

A creature revolting against a creator is revolting against the source of his own powers ... including even his power to revolt. ... It is like the scent of a flower trying to destroy the flower.
C. S. Lewis[1]

For I know that nothing good dwells in me, that is, in my flesh. For I have the desire to do what is right, but not the ability to carry it out. For I do not do the good I want, but the evil I do not want is what I keep on doing. Now if I do what I do not want, it is no longer I who do it, but sin that dwells within me.
Romans 7:18–20

"You're not the boss of me," our toddler exclaimed. He craned his neck to position his face two inches closer in my direction.

Standing less than thirty-six inches tall, his rally cry was clear. His defiant heels-dug-in little phrase and his posture were heart revealing. He let me know he was actively challenging my role as leader, Mom, and manager of his life.

If you're a parent, you've no doubt heard similar phrases and postures. The first time my son confronted me with defiant words or even silent resistance,

I honestly felt a bit amused. The very idea that this little person thought he could trump the authority of his dad or me was humorous.

However, these displays, which typically begin before our kids even speak, tell us much about the condition of their hidden hearts. Although they can certainly cause us to chuckle when they happen, they contain serious reminders that the heart is wayward, tainted, and diseased.

The Problem of Sin

We've discussed in detail how the eight heart cries of teens lead them to seek fulfillment in many ways—both positive and negative. In this chapter I want to explore an additional factor that drives teen attitudes and behavior: the problem of sin. You see, we all inherited a sin nature at birth. Sin is, in essence, rebelling against the authority of God—just as our toddlers rebelled against our leadership in the home.

I was amazed when my children demonstrated selfishness when I had modeled sharing. They had temper tantrums when they didn't get their way when obviously I knew what was best for them. I had shown self-sacrifice in attending to their needs, yet they displayed self-centeredness. They wanted more when I felt I had given everything.

Why do children lie with their hands caught in the proverbial cookie jar? Why do they want other children's toys, and bite, kick, and grab to get them? And then blame the other child for starting the fight?

God, our heavenly parent, sees these traits in all of us. He calls it a natural bent toward sin. I'll summarize in this chapter why we inherited a wayward heart and what God did about it. Then we'll discuss how our choice to receive or refuse His solution impacts meeting the eight heart cries native to all of us.

I'm aware that for some readers, this approach may seem backward or out of order. I wrestled with this issue for some time. I decided to focus on the wretchedly broken state of our kids' hearts in this last section rather than in the first. My choice rested on several factors I have encountered in my work with adolescents, young adults, and families.

First, many teens and parents are acutely aware of the reality of sin. They know the norms of good and bad behavior, and bad choices are almost always the reason I see them in my office. Often, I feel I must begin the counseling process on a more positive note. I try to help parents and teens understand that the heart core desires are powerful, beautiful, and empowering when approached in ways that God designed to fulfill them. Otherwise, they can be disabling.

Second, many families enter counseling with a goal of changing their adolescent's behavior. Nothing wrong with that desire. We love our kids and desperately want them to lead whole and healthy lives. That's why I first focus on heart core desires before venturing into the ins and outs of a wayward heart. I find the cravings that arise from the eight core desires serve as hooks or knobs by which caring adults can enter the sacred spaces of their hearts.

Once there—oh, how our God can use you in powerful ways to minister to the state of their hearts. I have seen Him do this time and time again in my relationships with kids and adults. I know He wants to use you, too, to be an instrument of His love, patience, mercy, wisdom, and guidance.

Third, I believe the wayward heart must be placed in the context of the four-part story that God has been writing from the beginning of time. If we understand this story, we can see how even harmless yearnings often lead to a myriad of harmful beliefs, choices, and lifestyles.

The next section will attempt to summarize this wondrous four-part story. Hopefully, it will be a story you will share with your family time and time again.

The Grand Narrative of Scripture

Have you ever sat down in the middle of a movie and tried to figure what happened before you tuned in? You might be able to deduce a few things from the unfolding actions on the screen. Likely, you'll miss the connection some of these have to the beginning of the drama. As a result, you may discount or even overlook the impact of the denouement or the surprising resolution at the end.

Similarly, we must not consider the state of the heart and the driving desires that reside there apart from the four chapters or movements of God's story. I like to call it HIStory. Otherwise, we're missing critical pieces that help us know how God's story interprets, confronts, reshapes, and redeems matters relating to the heart. While my brush strokes below are broad and incomplete, I hope they add enough color and detail to help you grasp how and why heart core desires tell us much about ourselves, our kids, and even more about our God.

Creation

The first chapter of this ongoing narrative can be called *Creation*. The story begins with a Trinitarian God—God the Father, the Son and the Holy Spirit—who eternally existed before all things. Then a day-by-day account shows that God literally spoke every aspect of creation into existence (Gen. 1:3-26). Last among God's formations were human beings created in His own image (Gen. 1:27).

Although man experienced the ultimate form of fellowship with his Creator, God fashioned for him a woman and declared, *It is not good that the man should be alone* (Gen. 2:18). God authored community so humans could create families. As they live together, they bear the image of and reflect the three-in-one God. God said He was pleased with all that he had made and declared humankind *very good* (Gen. 1:31).

In this garden of Eden world, the first couple flourished as they peacefully communed with God and each other. As mentioned in earlier chapters, humans were fully known in this perfect paradise. They never questioned whether their desire to be heard, noticed, affirmed, befriended, allowed, touched, protected, and remembered would go unnoticed or unsatisfied.

The Fall
Despite their *shalom* experience, the first humans entered the next chapter of the grand narrative, entitled *the Fall*. They chose to actively disobey God by moving beyond the limits He gave them. A serpent, embodying the evil one, deceived them by convincing them to doubt God's love, care, and goodness (Gen. 3:1–5). With phrases that began with, *Did God actually say,* and *You will not surely die,* the serpent lured them to want something beyond the safety, sustenance, and intimacy that God offered them.

The instant they ate from the Tree of the Knowledge of Good and Evil, sin entered the world. At that moment, Adam and Eve immediately experienced physical and emotional separation from one another. They noticed their nakedness and vulnerability and created a covering for themselves. Furthermore, in their shame, they hid from the Creator and blamed one another for their actions.

Because of this rebellious act, Adam and Eve—and by extension, the rest of humanity— experienced the curse of death resulting in emotional, physical, and spiritual separation from God (Gen. 3:22–24; Rom. 5:12). The curse of sin extended to all of the physical creation. Sinful humans living in a broken world are now infected by sin and susceptible to evil, deception, and destruction. Moreover, a sinful heart within us leads to fear, self-worship, and essentially pathological selfishness.

Our innate desire for self-rule, to build an identity apart from God, is evident well before a child insists on being "the boss of me." Paul David Tripp writes that since sin steals the worship and love that belong to God and gives it to something or someone else, it can be viewed as both "moral thievery" and "spiritual adultery."[2] This sinful heart is *deceitful above all things, and desperately sick* (Jer. 17:9).

Redemption

Despite the depth and breadth of man's pride and rebellion, our loving Creator God devised and implemented a master plan to redeem and rescue sinners. The third chapter of this drama of HIStory is entitled *Redemption*. To restore God's broken relationship with man, God sent His Son Jesus into the world to save us from the punishment of death we owe (Rom. 6:23).

On the cross Jesus paid the penalty for sin and thereby broke the dominion of sin over humankind (Col. 2:13–15). His sacrifice provides a way for humans to begin eternal fellowship with God and escape death (Gal. 3:13, 1 Cor. 15:22, 1 Pet. 2:24). The life, death, resurrection, and ascension of Jesus Christ is the definitive turning point of the grand narrative of the Bible.

Those who repent of their sins and place their faith in Jesus are deemed forgiven, righteous, and worthy to receive the inheritance of the Son— fellowship with God and eternal life (John 3:16; 1 Cor. 15:52–53). Justification, or payment for sin by Christ the Redeemer, was an act of grace and not a result of anything we have done or deserve (Eph. 2:8–9). The believer is filled by His Spirit and begins a transformative life with God here on Earth. Although still having a sin nature, the believer is empowered to overcome it through the Spirit's power (1 John 5:4).

The church, also known as the bride of Christ, becomes the embodiment of the gospel message. Within this community we experience and extend to others the very presence of Christ. The church and its members aren't perfect. As their lives become refined by Christ, they reflect Him. Through the church, individually and collectively, others can experience the hands, feet, and heart of Christ.

Restoration and Glorification

Thankfully, this glorious story doesn't end with redemption. In the final act, often referred to as *Restoration* or *Glorification*, Christ will return to judge sin and evil and create a new heaven and new earth. Jesus will have the final victory over Satan, thus purging the world of all evil (Rev. 20:10). His *shalom* will be re-established.

Those who have accepted Christ's sacrifice for their sins and thus been made new in Christ will be glorified—made like Him (1 John 3:2). In the book of Revelation, John gives us a glimpse of the glory and restoration that we await. No more sorrow, no more pain, no more death (Rev. 21:3–4). This final chapter provides a response to the injustices and inequalities experienced on Earth. Our present groanings—unmet desires—will finally be fulfilled in eternity with God.

Living between the third and fourth chapters of the grand narrative means that whether redeemed or not, we remain sinners residing alongside sinners in a broken and imperfect world. Until the coming age, Satan rules *the world,* or the system that remains in sinful opposition to God (1 John 5:19). Essentially, we can view him as the leader of an ongoing rebellion against God (John 12:31). He is determined to convince everyone—Jesus follower or not—that they should continue to doubt God and remain the ruler of their hearts.

How Desires Relate to the Narrative

With the grand narrative in mind, let's take a moment to connect key pieces of each of the four chapters with heart core desires and the related behaviors we see in our kids.

Creation

Recall that God created humankind to be fully satisfied in Him. His people would share perfect fellowship with God and with each other. Every heart core desire was designed with the capacity to be completely fulfilled.

Made in the image of God, your child's heart has within it a deep longing to experience intimacy without shame. It wants to know and be known by the Creator. Furthermore, this heart was made to experience aspects of the Godhead while in relationship with others. To be fully known and loved by God and to experience authentic connections with others remains knitted within the fibers of every human being.

At the very core, kids' ugly behaviors, disappointing decisions, and continual cravings for something more are evidence of unsatisfied deep needs. At the same time, they represent a beautiful desire that God stamped on their hearts to find sufficiency in Him.

The Fall

Humankind doubted God's word and His goodness to satisfy all of its desires. Rebelling against God's authority, we chose to idolize or worship something else. All sin has idolatry at its core.

Your kids' inherent sin nature will compel them to be the ruler of their hearts, to satisfy their desires in any way they see fit. Tripp writes:

While the object of their desire may not be evil at all, when not yielded to God these quickly turn into demands or survival needs ("I must" and "I deserve"). Each of these can produce expectations and eventually disappointment ("You should" and "You didn't") and possibly even punishment ("Because you didn't I will...").[3]

All of these outcomes represent the cycle within a heart enslaved, captured by sin. Because the captives deem themselves in charge of their hearts, they will always have the propensity to use anyone, even God, to try to make sure heart core desires are met.

Redemption

Because of the death and resurrection of Christ, we can have an eternally intimate, abiding, and sanctifying relationship with God. *Because of His promises and by His Spirit in us we can trust His goodness, His love, and His provision for our desires.*

Even if a kid accepts Christ's offer of redemption, being a new creature doesn't mean the heart stops longing. It also doesn't resolve our bent to sin, which continues to duel within us. However, yielding to Him daily means surrendering every choice to trust God's provision—through His Spirit, His word, His people—for the center place of the soul.

Some days, our kids' hearts will be full and overflowing with good attitudes and actions. Other days, they may seek to satisfy the heart core desires of others while their own longings remain unmet. God uses these moments and seasons to sustain, reveal, and ultimately remake your child into the likeness of Christ.

For those kids who don't know Christ as their personal Savior, an awareness of heart core desires during the adolescent years can often be the impetus that leads them to reflect on the possibility that there is a God, Jehovah-Jireh, our Provider. Furthermore, during this developmental season, many begin to recognize how people have failed to provide their deepest needs, leaving them feeling empty and unknown. They may be receptive to allowing God to give meaning and purpose to life.

Restoration or Glorification

At His second coming, Christ will conquer evil, create a new heaven and new earth, and thereby restore all things to His design. *Our hearts will be forever satisfied in Him once again.*

Oh, how our kids need to know that life on Earth is not the end of the story. While unsatisfied heart core desires will lead to ongoing discomfort and even pain, we can look forward to a life with God in heaven where our deepest longing to know and be known by God will forever be fully satisfied.

Because we currently reside between chapters three and four, our families—parents included—need to hear this story again and again. Our God-constructed hearts will never tire of hearing about His love and good intentions for His people. He desires to satisfy not only our greatest need—redemption and restoration—but also the daily longings that reside in the center place of the soul.

We must tell the story, talk about the story, and model the story so that our kids, through practice, will learn how to cling to Him and take risks in community.

The Battle for the Heart

In our imperfect homes in this broken world, our kids will be forever surrounded with the *marbles of this world*—the shiny substitutes of His plan, the promise for instant gratification, the immoral or impulsive decisions that leave them feeling more empty and heavy hearted. They will be tempted to quiet the cries within them in improper ways if they don't recognize they're living on a battlefield. The direction they face amidst the conflict—either toward or away from God—will influence not only what they believe and how they cope but also who they become.

I suppose we shouldn't be surprised that the intent of the snake's deceptive act in the garden boldly continues all around us today. He intends to question the limits and commandments God gave us. He breeds doubt about the goodness of our Creator. Satan—the enemy of God and slayer of hearts—uses smoke, mirrors, manipulation, or whatever means necessary to temporarily, and then permanently, deceive young people. Satan uses their growing awareness of heart core desires to convince them to buy into his destructive coping strategies.

Even if an adolescent has accepted Christ and yielded his life to Him, with the help of the Holy Spirit within him, he must still choose to battle the temptations Satan continually throws his way. While his relationship with God can't be severed, the enemy will do what he can to steer him away from Christ's lordship in order to disrupt the fellowship he has with the Lover of his heart.

In the midst of confusing or painful situations and disappointing relationships, the enemy will invite young women to zoom in on that which they lack so they can become increasingly obsessed with that which they desire. When they compare what they have to the seemingly perfect portraits of others, the emotions and the ache attached to wanting only intensifies. Once the emptiness surfaces, and if the enemy can kindle a bit of fear, anger, or jealousy, then he can permeate their minds with lies that overshadow the truths they may believe about God, the world, or themselves.

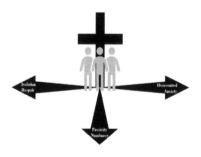

Diagram 7: *The enemy's strategy toward extremes*

At this point, the enemy of the heart uses many possible routes to steer teens away from the Maker of their hearts. As depicted in Diagram 7, the enemy likes to seduce the mind of adolescents to think in extremes. The extreme to the right describes the kid who is convinced to heighten being in control of his life and do whatever he needs to get what he wants. After all, he's now convinced he deserves it. The enemy tries to convince him to step it up and fight for what he wants. "Go get what you want, make it happen, rule your life," may be the kinds of messages he uses. Manipulation, aggression, and endless striving exist on this end of the spectrum.

By suppressing convictions and throwing out moral standards, teens may do what they desire to gain pleasure, instant gratification, and personal power. In my work with adolescents, the emotional state associated with this extreme is anxiety, fear, and restlessness. Sadly, the consequences may include physical and emotional destruction to self and/or others.

The left extreme involves the exact opposite. Here, the invitation of the enemy is to give up on relationships. This side is often associated with isolation or self-protection (think high walls) to prevent teens from experiencing more pain or repeated disappointments. The messages on this end convey a tone of shame and hatred toward self or others. Believing that either they or others aren't worthy of successful relationships, their reaction is to create emotional and physical distance from others.

These kids tell me two things: 1) People are stupid, or 2) I feel ridiculous or needy if I lean on others to satisfy the longings of my heart. The enemy loves to cement these beliefs by using painful memories from the past coupled with mental whispers such as *don't let them in, they will hurt you,* or *you aren't _____ enough anyway.* By viewing an inherent dependence on others as needy and unnecessary—or even as a sign of weakness—these kids may begin to construct a life of loneliness and/or contempt for others. They hope never to have to lean on others for help. Their dominant feeling is often depression while the action is withdrawal. The ultimate goal of the enemy is whatever it takes to keep them walking away from connection with others.

The final direction in which I see the enemy steer adolescents away from people (and the cross) is found below the figures in Diagram 7: to remain passive, checked out, and hopefully numb to their own desires and those of the people around them. Here Satan attempts to keep teens from making little to no movement at all. *Life is a crock so you might as well check out to endure it.* This is the underlying message for those lured to head in this direction.

For a variety of reasons, these kids have chosen to give up on themselves, others, and life in general. As a result, many often struggle with an overdependence on technology or substances. Both of these have been shown to lower motivation and increase anhedonia (an inability to feel pleasure). Cultural trends can really help the enemy keep these kids in limbo forever.

While there are a million different messages tailored just for your kid's heart, you can believe that the devil will do whatever he can to lure your kid down one or all of those paths in order to oppose the truths of the gospel and the hope of community. Furthermore, he remains fully aware of your child's unique weaknesses and her propensity toward sin. He knows how easy it is to cause the heart to wander and believe that life can really be found apart from God.

During the adolescent years, when heart core desires emerge and remain connected to so many developmental tasks, his deceitful messages easily intersect with satisfaction of the great eight heart cries. He knows that if he can convince teens to doubt or completely turn away from God, then they are likely to keep or replace the Ruler of their hearts with someone or something else. Whomever or whatever that is will quickly take the reins and thereby direct their thoughts and actions.

This battle doesn't just happen on occasion; it happens all day, every single day. Sadly, the very culture in which our kids are immersed generally affirms the overarching voice of the enemy. *Let your penchant for pleasure lead you away from other people, far away from the Author of pleasure, and toward whatever helps you cope with those menacing desires of the heart.*

In C.S. Lewis' brilliant novel, *The Screwtape Letters*, a senior demon writes to his nephew Wormwood, a young, inexperienced demon. Wormwood is charged with guiding a human away from "the enemy" (Jesus) and toward "Our Father Below" (the devil). He writes:

> I know we have won many a soul through pleasure. All the same, it is His invention, not ours. He made the pleasures: all our research so far has not enabled us to produce one. All we can do is to encourage the humans to take the pleasures which our Enemy has produced, at times, or in ways, or in degrees, which He has forbidden.[4]

Thankfully, the author of true, satisfying, and endless pleasure is far greater and much more powerful than the devil's plan.

God's plan is for adolescent longings, their desperate desires, and the resulting cries that accompany the pain and emptiness they experience to catapult them to the cross. There, as they sit in His presence, bathe in the truths of His word, and lean into people who mirror His heart, He can and will satisfy them ... in His perfect timing and in His perfect way.

Living Life in the Tension

Every restriction, boundary, or commandment the Lord gives us comes from God's commitment to the love and protection of His followers. He bids his people to steer clear of rebellious choices so they can avoid the wreckage that often follows these decisions. But trusting in God's provision and leaning into relationships can be hard when heart core desires regularly clamor for attention.

The temptation to take control and step outside of his limits—to lose hope or tune out in order to deal with the heart—causes measurable tension within most adolescents, even on a good day! Many of the kids I counsel tell me how tough it is to keep stepping toward God and/or community when they see or feel no change in their felt needs.

I often call this place of tension "the middle place"—that place where you don't feel fully satisfied, but you want to believe He is present, He is good, and He will provide. In Diagram 6, it's the land between all of the arrows. It's the place of community, where believers draw strength from each other. Believing adults experience this terrain often. But for adolescents this place of waiting while wanting can be distressing, even downright frightening. Their movement away from their dependence on parents or family to satisfy heart core desires makes this terrain even more challenging.

The moment when all heart core desires are satisfied on Earth is rare, if not impossible. I regularly tell teens that the *middle place* is really an everyday place. Whether they are believers or not, this land compels many to choose a path toward extremes. They aren't prepared. No one told them how uncomfortable it feels to take risks in relationships, to wait, or even to trust God when you don't see anything changing.

The kids I counsel who've made a commitment to Christ often believe that their hearts should never feel empty or unsatisfied. When flooded with these emotions, they don't know what to do. Some have been taught by example to fake it and act like all is well. Others believe they've done something wrong. Underneath their composed presence, they secretly feel shame and wonder what thoughts or actions led them to this state.

Sadly, many others will turn away from God and doubt His ability to sustain and satisfy. They may mirror the strategies of many of the unbelieving kids I counsel. They will bind their hearts to something other than God in the hope that this solution will rid them of the tension and distress that will always exist while living on this side of heaven.

C. S. Lewis addresses this issue so well in his classic book, *Mere Christianity*:

> If I find in myself a desire which no experience in this world can satisfy, the most probable explanation is that I was made for another world. If none of my earthly pleasures satisfy it, that does not prove that the universe is a fraud. Probably earthly pleasures were never meant to satisfy it, but only to arouse it, to suggest the real thing. If that is so, I must take care, on the one hand, never to despise, or to be unthankful

for, these earthly blessings, and on the other, never to mistake them for the something else of which they are only a kind of copy, or echo, or mirage. I must keep alive in myself the desire for my true country, which I shall not find till after death; I must never let it get snowed under or turned aside; I must make it the main object of life to press on to that country and to help others to do the same.[5]

These desires were made to point us to a great God, a great Giver, whose provisions never end and whose promises will prevail.

If you are willing to be one of those who help others distinguish between the real thing and the frauds that seek to satisfy earthly desires, the final chapter of this book is for you. First, I invite you to become a traveler-guide who is authentically walking the path of managing your own heart core desires. Second, you will simultaneously point a desirous teen toward a safe pathway that leads them homeward. It can be done. If you're ready for the call, then read on, my friend.

Chapter 14

A Guided Heart

When we love a person, we accept him or her exactly as is: the lovely with the unlovely, the strong with the fearful, the true mixed in with the façade, and of course, the only way we can do it is by accepting ourselves that way.
Fred Rogers[1]

But he said to me, "My grace is sufficient for you, for my power is made perfect in weakness." Therefore, I will boast all the more gladly of my weaknesses, so that the power of Christ may rest upon me.
2 Corinthians 12:9

O ur family loved to travel. My husband handled the reservations while I planned other attractions in the towns we visited. I often purchased a guidebook to help me get a better grasp of the place we were going to visit. These books seemed just a step away from having a tour guide whose personal experience offered direction, safety, and advice whenever we needed it.

If we found ourselves off the beaten path, I would read a few excerpts to help us decide our options.

When we weren't sure about where to dine, I consulted the book for suggestions. Once cell phones entered the scene, we relied heavily on GPS. But nothing compared to the pocket-sized city and metro maps when we needed to get our bearings. After visiting all thirty major league baseball stadiums in sixteen years, we learned a lot about baseball and ballparks from my husband. But our trusty little guidebooks gave us the wisdom we needed to better navigate the surrounding region.

If you've made it to this page in the book, I can confidently say that you, my friend, are a guidebook with skin on! Not many people understand the heart and the desires that flow from it. Most teens would benefit from the advice of a guide who knows a bit more than they do. Many are looking for a living guide who can point a lost or hurting kid in a safe direction. You can also provide a few suggestions and/ or warnings about how to cope with the relentless longings of the hidden heart.

One longitudinal study revealed that when parents commit to a posture of warmth, affection, and support during the adolescent years, they actually play a role in affecting the brain structure of their kids.[2] These changes unfold in regions of the brain frequently linked to lower rates of sadness, anxiety, and self-control. This protective factor vitally affects the brain's hardwiring, positively influencing the way kids cope with stressors across their lifespans.

Incredible, huh? God allows parents to positively influence who teens become just before they leave home. During a time in our country when so many teens are making destructive and deadly choices, this research underscores the importance of an empathetic and supportive guide to help teens better understand and manage the desires of their hearts.

A Qualified Traveler-Guide

At this point, I'm hoping you feel energized and motivated. However, like most parents and caring adults, you may also feel a bit overwhelmed and under qualified. Even though you've journeyed on this earth longer than your kids, you recognize your own limitations when it comes to understanding and leading the heart of another. After all, I started this book by establishing that the heart can indeed be quite mysterious and confusing.

While you may eagerly want to check the *yes* box regarding your desire to be a teen guide, perhaps your gut is saying, *how can I do this?* You've certainly not had every experience. If it helps at all, I want you to know that much of the time, I feel the same way. As a counselor, I know I've been called to be a heart guide. But, as a broken-hearted human and an imperfect mom, I often feel disqualified.

I've concluded the qualification for good guides lies in a willingness to acknowledge that you're a traveler, as well. Your heart feels, wants, dreams, and aches just like the one inside that teen you know. Continue to don both hats of a traveler and a guide, even if and when you get lost on your journey together. Your abiding commitment to the process—to being sensitive to the needs, wants, and desires of the one you're leading—will often be all you need to make it to your destination.

Being a traveler-guide parallels a few of the attributes found in that brain-changing group of parents in the study. Every kid I've met deeply desires someone who is willing to walk alongside them. The decisions related to their desires may threaten to unravel your own heart. When your heart actually unravels, you're still qualified. In fact, you've just increased your qualifications.

The Heart of the Traveler-Guide

When I sit with families or speak to audiences about these unending desires of the heart, I often see a combination of curiosity and confirmation on the faces in the group. Curiosity prevails as I begin to explain heart core desires. As we progress, sometimes ah's and nods are replaced with faces of confusion and even despair. Despite my desire to offer ways that parents can practically respond to a teen's heart core desires, many tell me they feel overwhelmed.

"How can I care for her heart when mine is full of desire as well?"

"Why does his heart take center stage while mine is backstage dying?"

"I am so tired of trying, my heart has little to no reserves left because of other stressors in my life."

Parenting adolescents makes us aware of our own unmet needs. After devoting so much time and energy to marriage, kids, work, and possibly extended family and friends, many parents I meet have unknowingly neglected their own hearts in the process. They've moved from one crisis to another and overlooked the very part of them that's central to solving the many dilemmas they'll face as parents and/or caregivers. This neglect or denial of self-care only exacerbates their exhaustion.

I really do understand why that disheartened sigh slips out. Now they've discovered that the state of their own hearts can positively or negatively influence the state of their kids' hearts. The information must feel like an invitation to go on a trip to Kathmandu with no experience, no money, no map, and very little sleep. Over time, you will find that as you pay attention to the stirrings in your heart, guiding a teen's heart will unfold far more easily. If they see you caring for your heart cries in a way that helps, they can learn to manage theirs. I'm sure you know this by now, but most teenagers are better observers and imitators than listeners.

Caring for Your Heart Needs

If you'll recall from the first section of the book, I presented Diagram 3, Heart in the Soul. It offers a broad understanding of the importance of heart core desires, particularly during adolescent development. Adult development isn't as intricately tethered to the way we satisfy heart core desires. However, the state of your soul at any given time will always be affected by these longings.

Even now, as you are reading this last chapter, I'm pretty certain that in the past few hours or days one of your heart core desires clamored for attention. Perhaps you felt misunderstood, devalued, or completely unnoticed. If you tuned in to your heart, then you know that the experience, however big or small, inevitably provoked core beliefs to arise. They impacted your thoughts, actions, and inactions—even your attitudes and the way your body felt.

You may have dealt with this pang by reaching out toward others and talking about it. Maybe you vented to a friend or cried with a spouse. You might have had a conversation with God about your heart. Perhaps you did none of that and chose to distract yourself, dismiss the ripple effect, and/or deny the pain altogether.

Whatever your response, I want to emphasize that the best traveler-guides are willing to grow in their awareness of how the eight core desires show up and impact their own lives. The reason for this is two-fold. First, they've learned that heart cries deeply matter.

By paying attention to the center of their own souls, they're more attuned to the way their inner person (heart) and outer person (body and behavior) influence or disrupt one another. This awareness hopefully makes them more willing to reach outward or upward as needed to care for their own unmet needs. Second, they're better equipped to understand the complexities of their teens' hearts and more compassionate toward them.

A Practice Exercise

To move this connection from just a good idea to a helpful practice, let's take a minute and review the list of heart core desires that reside in you, the traveler-guide.

> *Hear me! Notice me! Affirm me! Befriend me!*
> *Allow me! Touch me! Protect me! Remember me!*

Which one of these quickened your heart a bit? If you didn't feel it, then read the list again, slowly. Which seemed to draw your attention the most? Which of these may lie beneath some of your best and worst actions or decisions in the last few days? Write down the desire and the thoughts, feelings, actions, and physical sensations connected to it. Reach out and entrust your heart to a trusted relative or friend by sharing what you are experiencing in your own heart.

After considering the one or two that matter most, lean in to the biblical truths related to these. I've included two in each chapter on heart cries. How thankful I am that God has much more to say about each of these. Carry on a conversation with the One who designed your heart, the One who orchestrated desire, and the One who knows how to minister to your heart in the most surprising and satisfying ways.

As you learned in Chapter 12, our wounds impact the way we cope with and satisfy heart core desires. Emptiness today reminds us of the *not enoughs* from other days. People have disappointed you. Relationships have been lacking, limited, or perhaps languishing over the years. Even if a rupture has been repaired, our social—yet protective—brain and body is wired to remember and remind us so that we don't let it happen again.

Old wounds such as loss/abandonment, rejection, humiliation/criticism, and betrayal are triggered in so many ways. Just the feelings associated with an empty, unsatisfied heart are all the brain needs to resort to protective practices. These minimize the discomfort and attempt to shield us from the hurt.

Regardless of whether you deny, disconnect, or distract yourself when you are triggered, a traveler-guide's commitment to know her story, recognize when wounds have been activated, and share this pain with safe persons can make all the difference. Your power over your story increases when it's exposed and meaningfully incorporated into your narrative. Conversely, the painful events of your story will repeatedly overpower you when they remain hidden and disconnected from your overall narrative. Exposing pain harvests hope; hiding it fuels shame.

Modeling the Process

Because most parents understandably desire to shield their kids from the pain of their past, many adolescents don't get to see how an adult deals with a wound when it's triggered. Contrast that reality to the many examples they have in their peer population, as well as in the media and on the Internet.

While I don't recommend that we turn to our kids to help us sort through our wounds and coping mechanisms, when we are able to talk openly about pieces of our struggle, they assimilate several things. First, they recognize that we might understand their pain because we hurt, too. Second, they benefit from the empathy that flows from identifying with our past. Third, when we deal with some of our pain before their eyes, they get to see a parent intentionally implement healthy and hope-filled strategies. Yes, this is exhausting and confusing and messy and doesn't always offer the example that we hope for. But isn't that part of being an authentic human being?

For many reasons, even as a counselor, I can only share a protected and rather limited portfolio of my wounds and coping mechanisms with clients. As a result, adolescents benefit from seeing how the people who care for them day in and day out deal with the junk that arises in and around them. Although this may feel uncomfortable and unnatural, sharing our journey is part of being a traveler-guide. It offers a snapshot of what it looks like to keep your heart connected and alive even in the midst of treacherous and painful terrain.

Perfectly Imperfect Traveler-Guides

I have no memories of perfect family trips. Even when it seemed we had prepared for everything, something inevitably went awry on every vacation. The most intrusive and memorable glitches tried our patience and tested our relationships. These seemed to fall into two categories—disruptions from the outside or disturbances from the inside.

Disruptions included unpredictable annoyances like plane cancellations, lost reservations, misplaced personal items, or sudden car issues. Disturbances included the extreme and often irrational reactions to a disruption. But they also encompassed the irritable temperaments and sudden moodiness that surface when people journey together.

C.S. Lewis wisely noted, "Everyone feels benevolent if nothing happens to be annoying him at the moment."[3] How fitting these words as we consider the journey we're on. Care and compassion come easily when nothing triggers you. It's how you deal with the disruptions and disturbances that matter most.

As you commit to the task of being a traveler-guide by recognizing, responding, and relaying truths about heart core desires to your kids, realize that the best-laid plans will never be enough. The journey ahead will be filled with unexpected challenges, disheartening situations, and a myriad of disappointments. No manual or amount of preparation can fully prepare you for the tough terrain you and your kids will cover as you keep the heart in mind.

What I continue to remember as a mom and counselor is that the most disruptive and disagreeable moments actually offer us memorable learning experiences. After all, when kids reveal raw emotions, you're most likely on the other side of their protective walls. You're seeing and feeling the authentic state of their hearts. If you can begin to view these disruptions as opportunities that literally catapult you into a sacred space—the center of their souls—then you might just work a little harder to replace your immediate reaction with a wiser, slower, and gentler approach.

Unfortunately, when raw emotions suddenly surface, the experience typically throws you into more of a reactive than a receptive state. You may feel exhausted or empty. But, here's the thing. These occurrences don't happen by accident. Although we may view them as the blind heart leading the blind heart, I prefer to view them as the weak traveler-guide leading the weak traveler. Both are desperately in need of something greater than themselves. Both long to be satisfied. Yet one has been given both the call and authority to lead the other. And the other hopes they will answer the call.

Biblical Models of Traveler-Guides

When raw emotions erupt, you will sometimes mess up. If you extend yourself some grace and ultimately focus on how you can reconnect with each other after the scene, you won't be very different than the heroes of the faith. Think about Moses, Nehemiah, David, Ruth, Esther and even Mary. Though each of them displayed differing strengths as they travelled their specific terrains, we can relate to their humanity. They were men and women with weaknesses and struggles. While you may not always see yourself as heroic, I think the two important elements that mark each of their stories shorten the distance between them and us.

They Answered the Call

The first was their willingness to say *yes* to the challenges they were given. Consider Moses. If you look at his early years, you'll quickly note more about him that appears to disqualify rather than qualify him for God's call. Growing up in an Egyptian palace, his upbringing was completely unlike those he was called to lead (Ex. 2:10, 14). He was privileged, yet they were commoners. You have to wonder if this traveler-guide struggled to relate to those in slavery.

We also know that Moses wasn't a great communicator. In fact, he begged God to send someone else to speak to the Israelites (Ex. 4:10–14). He probably doubted that anything he would say could make sense. Oh my, how I often feel that way in my work with teens! Also, we learn from Scripture that Moses could be a bit reactive—or some might even say hot-tempered (Ex. 2:12; Num. 20:11). Stubborn and impatient people got the best of him on more than one occasion. Yep, I can relate to that one too. Adolescents can push hot buttons in me.

Finally, did you know that before Moses received his call from God, the few lines that appear in the biblical narrative are questions? (Ex. 2:13, 3:11) Moses was curious. He didn't pretend to know it all. Despite the fact that Moses couldn't always relate, communicate, remain calm, or know every answer, God still invited him to co-labor with Him. He led his people on the journey of their lives. It began when imperfect Moses said *yes* to a call that was bigger than he.

Their Tender Hearts Mirrored God's Heart
The second attribute that exists within the long list of traveler-guides who've gone before us lies in the state of their hearts. John Maxwell says it well when he writes, "To measure a leader, put a tape around his heart, not his head."[4]

When Samuel was looking for a new king, the Lord said to him, *Do not look on his appearance or on the height of his stature, because I have rejected him. For the Lord sees not as man sees: man looks on the outward appearance, but the Lord looks on the heart* (1 Sam. 16:7). David didn't need a poised posture or a confident carriage to be used by God. Instead, his humble heart impacted those around him. We remember David for having a heart like God's heart (1 Sam. 13:14).

Nehemiah also comes to mind. Upon hearing about the plight of his people in Jerusalem, he *sat down and wept and mourned for days ... fasting and praying before the God of heaven* (Neh. 1:4). Nehemiah imagined their plight and allowed the tears to flow. His heart mirrored God's grieving heart. I believe a tender heart actually empowers many great traveler-guides to say *yes* to the challenges they face.

Even though Nehemiah clearly saw the extensive mess, he didn't rebuke the people. Instead, he considered their problem as his problem. He said: *You see the trouble we are in, how Jerusalem lies in ruins with its gates burned. Come, let us build the wall of Jerusalem, that we may no longer suffer derision* (Neh. 2:17). At the conclusion of the book of Nehemiah, his heart is revealed through his final plea: *Remember me, O my God, for good* (Neh. 13:31). Even after all he had accomplished, Nehemiah sought God alone to satisfy his own heart core desire to be remembered. What a remarkable reminder that he, too, was a traveler as well as a guide.

Unpredictable Territory Lies Ahead

A willingness to say *yes* to being a guide, plus a tender traveler's heart, yields to God's plan even when the path is unknown and unpredictable. Repeatedly, I have seen these two factors empower many adults to guide and deeply connect with the heart of a teen. Like the leaders mentioned in the Bible, the journey never resembles a Hallmark movie. The challenges they faced were often overwhelming. Many never saw the complete result. In fact, many dealt with a lot of complaining, belittling, staring, questioning, bickering, and disinterest.

Does that sound familiar? Just because you're called to be a traveler-guide doesn't mean that every teen you lead will embrace the idea of your pursuit of his heart. The reason is threefold: your pursuit essentially requires him to accept *exposure, dependence,* and *redirection.*

Exposing the heart can feel like you're placing a floodlight on every wounded and broken part of them. Their response requires vulnerability to let you see inside. *Dependence* means they must suppress their innate impulse to remain self-sufficient and independent. Reaching out and leaning on others requires courage. It's humbling to anyone to acknowledge they're lost or incompetent. *Redirection* requires listening to and then accepting your suggestions about satisfying their hearts in other, more fruitful ways.

As you prove you're a safe person, one who's willing to sit with them in their pain instead of judging it or shutting it down, most adolescents will allow you to lead. It just takes time, persistence, and an indefinable amount of patience.

Because of the tumult of the heart during adolescence, we must remember that even our best intentions might be met with a great deal of resistance. I urge you not to get discouraged or overwhelmed by their response, whatever it is. What most kids fear more than the reveal itself is what you will do or say immediately afterward. Will you laugh? Will you dismiss or minimize their pain? Will you tell everyone? Will you convince them that they shouldn't feel that way? The shame, belittling, or condemnation they expect for the doing, needing, wanting, and wishing they experience keeps so many kids from letting others in.

Brene Brown, a vulnerability researcher, writes, "Shame, blame, disrespect, betrayal, and the withholding of affection damage the roots from which love grows."[5] This means that the most important role you play as a traveler-guide lies in your commitment to ensure that those roots remain alive. Allow your heart to feel what they feel while mentally staying grounded in truth. I know. This is hard work. And it's taxing and terrifying—yet totally worth it.

Even though most teens appear more interested in the opinions of their peers—or even people they've never met—than in yours, their traveler-guides, your voice and your presence undeniably have the most power. On the one hand, this means that if you choose to dismiss their hearts (or your own), you will indirectly teach them to dismiss and devalue the happenings of their hearts. Worse yet, because of your influence, you play a lasting role in what meaning they take with them from their experience with you.

On the other hand, if you acknowledge and speak life into their heart core desires, you are ultimately helping them decode the complexities of their hearts. You imbue these desires with meaning. This is critical. We've known for some time that it's not so much the negative experiences that shape the well-being of an individual but how they remember and interpret them.[6] As a traveler-guide, you're an interpreter, a meaning maker. Even if a teen dismisses or even demeans your gentle pursuit, recognize that your willingness to engage with them powerfully affects the reality they are constructing about their experience.

You're Not Alone

When God places a call on people's lives, He never expects them to do the work alone. The leaders in the Old Testament knew how dependent they had to be upon God. The same was true of Jesus when He called the disciples. They didn't know all of the details. They focused on the fact that living and working alongside Jesus *was far more valuable than being able to see the entire road ahead.*

I know it might not always seem this way, but there are many traveler-guides among you. I meet many parents who are working hard to stay committed, engaged, and involved with their adolescents throughout the high school and college years. Those who are doing it right are experiencing highs as well as many lows. You might not always find these people on your social media feeds. And, sadly, they might not always be easy to locate in a church. They may feel judged by others if they speak up. But these parents are out there.

Perhaps sharing your struggles with someone in your neighborhood, at work, or in church might be a starting place for you. Sometimes, finding an older parent who has successfully travelled to the other side of parenting adolescents might be the best option. Be willing to move beyond parenting *behavior* in order to parent *the heart.* Then you will really need to link arms with several parents who are committed to parenting the hearts of their kids.

Becoming a traveler-guide who is committed to create pathways that may enable a kid to lean into both his community and Christ is indisputably His work, my friend. When the heart remains open, honest, connected to community, and yielded to Christ, He is glorified. He won't leave you alone because He's frankly more interested in the life of the heart than you or I ever will be. He might not reveal the path immediately or resolve today's challenges, but He will always provide you with just what you need.

Jesus said: *My grace is sufficient for you, for my power is made perfect in weakness"* (2 Cor. 12:9). When we say *yes* and entrust our own hearts to Him, His grace and unending presence is sufficient. You are His. He is yours. He's holding you, helping you, leading you, grieving with you, and even chuckling with you. Know that you're in the palm of His hand, as you remain engaged in work that's near and dear to the Father's heart.

When our kids were younger, we ended their day by singing them a blessing song. I can think of no other way to end this book than by leaving you with a portion of the melody we sang each night to the child that gracefully ushered us into parenting adolescents.

The LORD bless you and keep you;

the LORD make his face to shine upon you and be gracious to you;

the LORD lift up his countenance upon you and give you peace.

Numbers 6:24–26

Endnotes

Chapter 1

1. Robert S. McGee, *The Search for Significance Book and Workbook* (Nashville, TN: Thomas Nelson Publishers, 2003), 11.

2. "Heart," *Baker's Evangelical Dictionary of Biblical Theology,* http://www.biblestudytools.com/dictionaries/bakers-evangelical-dictionary/heart.html.

3. W.E. Vine, Merrill F. Unger, and William White, Jr., *Vine's Complete Expository Dictionary of Old and New Testament Words* (Nashville, TN: Thomas Nelson Publishers, 1996), 108-109.

4. Frederick Buechner, "Introduction," *Telling Secrets* (New York, NY: HarperCollins Publisher, 1991), 2-3.

Chapter 2

1. John Ortberg, *Soul Keeping* (Michigan: Zondervan, 2014), 100.

2. Dallas Willard, *Renovation of the Heart: Putting on the Character of Christ* (Colorado Springs, CO: NavPress, 2002), 199.

3. Ibid, 273.

4. C.S. Lewis, *The Problem of Pain* (New York: Harper-CollinsPublishers, 2001), 91.

Chapter 3

1. Carol Burnett, http://www.brainyquote.com/quotes/authors/c/carol_burnett.html.

2. D. J. Flannery, D. C. Rowe, and B. L. Gulley, "Impact of pubertal status, timing, and age on adolescent sexual experience and delinquency," *Journal of Adolescent Research*, Vol. 8, (1993), 21–40.

3. B. J. Casey, R. M. Jones, and T. A. Hare, "The Adolescent Brain," *Annals of the New York Academy of Sciences*, Vol. *1124*, (2008), 111–126. http://doi.org/10.1196/annals.1440.010

Chapter 4

1. Patrick Ness, *The Rest of Us Just Live Here*, http://www.goodreads.com/quotes/tag/adolescence.

2. C.S. Lewis, *Collected Letters of CS Lewis*, Vol. 3 (San Francisco, CA: Harper San Francisco, 2007), 1102.

3. Paul David Tripp, *Age of Opportunity: A Biblical Guide to Parenting Teens* (Phillipsburg, NJ: P&R, 2001), 226.

Chapter 5

1. John Piper, https://www.desiringgod.org/messages/god-has-chosen-us-in-him-before-the-foundation-of-the-earth

2. Curt Thompson, *The Soul of Shame: Retelling the Stories We Believe About Ourselves* (Illinois: InterVarsity Press, 2015), 138.

3. Richard Rohr, *Falling Upward: A Spirituality for the Two Halves of Life* (California: Jossey-Bass, 2011), 159.

4. Erika Morrison, *Bandersnatch: An Invitation to Explore Your Unconventional Soul* (Tennessee: Thomas Nelson, 2015), 32.

5. Pew Research Center, www.pewinternet. org/2015/10/01/teens-technology-and-romantic-relationships/

6. Elizabeth Mumford and Bruce Taylor, *National Survey on Teen Relationships and Intimate Violence (STRiV)* (2014) NORC, Chicago.

7. Kare Anderson, "What Captures Your Attention Controls Your Life," *Harvard Business Review* (June 5, 2012), https://hbr.org/2012/06/what-captures-your-attention-c

8. Charles Spurgeon, Sermon 232. January 2, 1859, New Park Street Chapel, Southwark, England.

Chapter 6

1. Abraham Lincoln, http://www.quotationspage. com/quotes/Abraham_Lincoln.

2. Nathaniel Branden, *The Psychology of Self-Esteem: A New Concept of Man's Psychological Nature* (Los Angeles, CA: Nash Publishing, 1969), 4.

3. Roy F. Baumeister, Jennifer D. Campbell, Joachim I. Kruegger, and Kathleen D.Vohs, "Does High Self-Esteem Cause Better Performance, Interpersonal Success, Happiness, or Healthier Lifestyles?" *Psychological Science in the Public Interest,* Vol. 4 (May 2003), 38-39.

4. Jean Twenge, *Generation Me: Why Today's Young Americans Are More Confident, Assertive, Entitled— And More Miserable than Ever Before* (New York: Free Press, 2006), 106-108.

5. S. K. Bearman, E. Martinez, E. Stice, and K. Presnell, "The Skinny on Body Dissatisfaction: A Longitudinal Study of Adolescent Girls and Boys," *Journal of Youth and Adolescence, 35* (2) (April 2006), 217, http://doi.org/10.1007/s10964-005-9010-9.

6. Robert S. McGee, *The Complete Search for Significance* (Houston, TX: Rapha Publishing, 1994), 116.

Chapter 7

1. Stephen Marche, "Is Facebook Making Us Lonely?" www.theatlantic.com *(May, 2012);* http://www.theatlantic.com/magazine/archive/2012/05/is-facebook-making-us-lonely/308930/.

2. Dave Evans, "The Internet of Things: How the Next Evolution of the Internet Is Changing Everything," *Cisco's Internet Business Solutions Group* (IBSG, 2011), 2-3, https://www.cisco.com/c/dam/en_us/about/ac79/docs/innov/IoT_IBSG_0411FINAL.pdf.

3. John T. Cacioppo, James H. Fowler, and Nicholas A. Christakis, "Alone in the Crowd: The Structure and Spread of Loneliness in a Large Social Network," *Journal of Personality and Social Psychology*, 2006; http://www.ncbi.nlm.nih.gov/pmc/articles/PMC2792572/.

4. http://www.pewinternet.org/2015/04/09/teens-social-media-technology-2015/pi_2015-04-09_teensandtech_06/

5. http://www.pewinternet.org/fact-sheets/broadband-technology-fact-sheet/

6. Executive Summary: The Common Sense Census: Media Use by Tweens and Teens, http://www.commonsensemedia.org/sites/default/files/uploads/research/census_executive summary.pdf

7. Stephen Marche, *Ibid.*

8. Sherry Turkle, TED2012: "Connected, but Alone?" February 2012 (12:07; see transcript link at https://www.ted.com/talks/sherry_turkle_alone_together/transcript?language=en.

Chapter 8

1. Timothy Keller and Katherine Leary Alsdorf, *Every Good Endeavor: Connecting Your Work to God's Work* (New York: Riverhead Books, 2012), p. 24.

2. Jeffrey Jensen Arnett, "G. Stanley Hall's Adolescence: Brilliance and Nonsense," *History of Psychology 2006*, Vol. 9, No. 3, 186-187.

3. Robert Epstein, *Teen 2.0, Saving Our Children and Families from the Torment of Adolescence* (Fresno, CA: Quill Driver Books, 2010), 29-30.

4. Ibid, 402.

5. Laurence Steinberg, "A social neuroscience perspective on adolescent risk taking," *Developmental Review*, 2008, Vol. 28 No. 1; 99; Retrieved from: http://www.sciencedirect.com/science/article/pii/S0273229707000536.

6. Keller and Alsdorf, 107.

Chapter 9

1. Tiffany Field, *Touch* (Cambridge, Mass: MIT Press, 2001), 35.

2. Michael W. Krass, Cassy Huang, and Dacher Keltner, "Tactile Communication, Cooperation and Performance: An Ethological Study of the NBA," (2010) *American Psychologist*, 10 (5), 745-749.

3. "National Survey of Reproductive and Contraceptive Knowledge," (2009) *The National Campaign to Prevent Teen and Unplanned Pregnancy*, https://www.guttmacher.org/population-center/dataset/2009-national-survey-reproductive-and-contraceptive-knowledge

4. http://www.familysafemedia.com/pornography_statistics.html.

5. TruResearch (2012) Covenant Eyes, 2015, Pornography Statistics at http://www.covenanteyes.com/lemonade/wp-content/uploads/2013/02/2015-porn-stats-, www.covenant-eyes.pdf

6. Jason S. Carroll, *et al*, "Generation XXX: Pornography Acceptance and Use Among Emerging Adults, *Journal of Adolescent Research* 23.1 (2008), 6-30. Study examined population of emerging adults, aged 18-26.

7. https://www.webroot.com/us/en/resources/tips-articles/internet-pornography-by-the-numbers

8. James W. Prescott, "Body Pleasure and the Origins of Violence," *Bulletin of the Atomic Scientists* (1975), 10-20.

9. https://www.cdc.gov/mmwr/preview/mmwrhtml/mm6227a1.htm.

10. Miguel A. Diego, *et al*, "Aggressive Adolescents Benefit from Massage Therapy," *Adolescence*, vol. 37, no. 147, (2002), 597.

11. Virginia Satir, quoted in "9 Reasons You Need To Be Giving and Receiving Hugs Everyday" by Josh Richardson, Jan. 23, 2014, http://preventdisease.com/news/14/012314_9-Reasons-Need-Giving-Receiving-Hugs-Everyday.shtml.

12. R.W. Blum and P.M. Rinehart (1998), "Reducing the risk: Connections that make a difference in the lives of youth," *Center for Adolescent Health and Development*, University of Minnesota. Minneapolis, MN.

Chapter 10

1. Dillon Burroughs, *Hunger No More Devotional*, October 2, 2018 (Kindle).

2. Fast Facts: National Center for Education Statistics (2013) https://www.nces.ed.gov/fastfacts/display.asp?id=719

3. S.T. Lereya, *et al*, (2013) "Being bullied during childhood and the prospective pathways to self-harm in late adolescence," *Journal of the American Academy of Child and Adolescent Psychiatry*, 52 (6).

4. John Townsend, *Boundaries with Teens: When to Say Yes, How to Say No* (Grand Rapids: Zondervan, 2006), 35.

5. "Surveillance Summaries: Youth Risk Behavior Surveillance-United States, 2013, PDF" *Center for Disease Control,* MMWR (2014) 63 (no. SS-4).

6. Corrie ten Boom, *The Hiding Place* (New Jersey: Fleming H. Revell, 1971), 53.

Chapter 11

1. Timothy Keller, *Every Good Endeavor: Connecting Your Work to God's Work,* https://www.goodreads.com/quotes/752418-everyone-will-be-forgotten.

2. Joseph Campbell, *The Hero with a Thousand Faces,* 2nd Ed. (Princeton, N.J.: Princeton University Press, 1972).

3. https://www.barna.org/barna-update/donors-cause/22-despite-benefits-few-americans-have-experienced-short-term-mission-trips#.V3_8GL-grl2w

Chapter 12

1. https://www.goodreads.com/quotes/search?utf8=✓&q=mental+pain&commit=Search

2. Ronald Brill, (2000), "Emotional Honesty and Self-Acceptance: Education Strategies for Preventing violence," Xlibris Corporation.

3. C.S. Lewis, "The Weight of Glory," *Screwtape Proposes a Toast* (London: Collins, 1965), 97-98.

4. https://d3uet6ae1sqvww.cloudfront.net/pdf/discovery-series/when-trust-is-lost-healing-for-victims-of-sexual-abuse.pdf; p. 8.

5. Bessel A. van der Kolk, *The Body Keeps the Score: Brain, Mind, and Body in the Healing of Trauma* (NY: Penguin Books, 2014), p. 97.

6. "Drugs, brains, and behavior: The science of addiction," *National Institute of Drug Abuse* NIH publication no. 08-5605, 2008.

Chapter 13

1. https://www.goodreads.com/quotes/search?utf8=✓&q=mental+pain&commit=Search

2. Ronald Brill. (2000) Emotional Honesty and Self-Acceptance: Education Strategies for Preventing violence. Xlibris Corporation.

3. C.S. Lewis. "The Weight of Glory," in *Screwtape Proposes a Toast* (London: Collins, 1965), 97-98.

4. https://d3uet6ae1sqvww.cloudfront.net/pdf/discovery-series/when-trust-is-lost-healing-for-victims-of-sexual-abuse.pdf, p. 8.

5. Bessel A. van der Kolk, *The Body Keeps the Score: Brain, Mind, and Body in the Healing of Trauma* (NY: Penguin Books, 2014), p. 97.

6. C.S. Lewis, *Mere Christianity* (New York: HarperOne, 1952), 136-137.

Chapter 14

1. Fred Rogers, *You are special: Words of wisdom for all ages from a beloved neighbor* (New York, NY: Penguin Books, 1995), 13.

2. S. Whittle, J. G. Simmons, M. Dennison, N. Vijaya-kumar, O. Schwartz, M. B Yap, L. Sheeber, N.B. Allen, "Positive parenting predicts the development of adolescent neural reward circuitry: A longitudinal study," *Frontiers in Human Neuroscience*, 2003, 7. http://doi:10.3389/conf.fnhum.2013.212.00074.

3. C. S. Lewis, *The problem of pain* (London: Collins, 2012), 8.

4. J. C. Maxwell, *The Right to Lead: Learning Leadership Through Character and Courage* (Nashville: Thomas Nelson, Inc., 2010), 75.

5. B. Brown, *Daring Greatly: How the Courage to Be Vulnerable Transforms the Way We Live, Love, Parent, and Lead* (New York: Penguin, 2012), 93.

6. D. Kahneman and E. Diener, eds., *Well-Being: Foundations of Hedonic Psychology* (Plymouth: Rowman & Littlefield Publishing Group, 2003), 3-25.

About the Author

Jackie Perry has worked as an adolescent and family therapist for 27 years. She is married to her college sweetheart, John, and together they have three adult children. She feels blessed to call Asheville, North Carolina, home. She is an adjunct faculty member in the graduate department at Lenoir Rhyne University.

Jackie is a graduate of Duke University and is pursuing a Ph.D. in Counselor Education and Supervision at Regent University. Her writing companion is the family dog, Bailey, a mini goldendoodle, who loves an occasional rub or walk in the woods near their house.

Jackie considers the perfect day to be a combination of a hike culminating with a view of the Blue Ridge Mountains followed by a cozy evening hanging out with her family or reading one of the books stacked on her nightstand. She is happy to be able to say, "I did it!" to two very important challenges in her life—raising teenagers and writing her first book!